Praise for *Short-chang*

"South Africa is a place
The past is always palpa
exceptionally thoughtfu.   ₒₗ ₜₕₑ country's
most distinguished historians, Colin Bundy, explains
quite how much this is true. For all its brevity, *Short-
changed?* packs a hefty punch: not only does it offer a
compelling explanation for the fall of apartheid, but
it makes a very persuasive case for the ways in which
the long shadow of colonialism has insinuated itself,
is insinuating itself, into the South African here-and-
now—and into its probable futures."

—John Comaroff, co-author of *Theory from the South:
Or, How Euro-America Is Evolving toward Africa.*

"In *Short-changed? South Africa since Apartheid,* Colin
Bundy provides a powerfully incisive analysis of how
the past continues to reverberate in post-apartheid
South Africa. He also shows how the prospects for
change hinge crucially on confronting the legacies of
the past."

—Gillian Hart, author of
Rethinking the South African Crisis

"This is a morally charged contemporary politics as
read by one of South Africa's major historians. For

Colin Bundy's argument is that notwithstanding major reforms, South Africa's past still helps to configure political, economic, and social life in fundamental ways. . . . In this powerful text, measured assessment is balanced by moral conviction. [It] is luminous contemporary history."

—Tom Lodge, author of *Sharpeville:*
An Apartheid Massacre and Its Consequences

"Insightful and thoughtful throughout, this judicious assessment clarifies the problems facing post-apartheid South Africa with precision and care. I know of no better historically informed introduction to the state of the nation."

—Saul Dubow, author of
South Africa's Struggle for Human Rights

"Bundy's lively and deeply insightful book demonstrates the importance of historical analysis for those who wish to understand contemporary South Africa. Bundy shows that the country's past continues to cast a long shadow over her present; and he argues that the dangers and opportunities that the future holds can only be understood in the context of long-range patterns of accumulation and exploitation."

—Anthony Butler, University of Cape Town

Short-changed?

OHIO SHORT HISTORIES OF AFRICA

This series of Ohio Short Histories of Africa is meant for those who are looking for a brief but lively introduction to a wide range of topics in African history, politics, and biography, written by some of the leading experts in their fields.

Short-changed?

South Africa since Apartheid

Colin Bundy

OHIO UNIVERSITY PRESS

ATHENS, OHIO

Ohio University Press, Athens, Ohio 45701
www.ohioswallow.com
All rights reserved

First published by Jacana Media (Pty) Ltd in 2014
10 Orange Street
Sunnyside
Auckland Park 2092
South Africa
+27 011 628 3200
www.jacana.co.za

To obtain permission to quote, reprint, or otherwise reproduce
or distribute material from Ohio University Press publications,
please contact our rights and permissions department at (740)
593-1154 or (740) 593-4536 (fax).

First published in North America in 2015 by Ohio University Press
Printed in the United States of America
Ohio University Press books are printed on acid-free paper ⊗ ™

ISBN: 978-0-8214-2155-0
e-ISBN: 978-0-8214-4525-9

Library of Congress Cataloging-in-Publication Data available

Cover design by Joey Hi-Fi

Contents

Acknowledgements

This little book first took shape as a series of lectures in the 2013 Summer School at the University of Cape Town. I am grateful to Ingrid Fiske and Medee Rall for their encouragement and to their colleagues, especially Fezile Kama, for being unfailingly helpful. The final session of the summer school class was a panel discussion: Judith February, Ronnie Kasrils and Xolela Mangcu made it a memorable evening. I enjoyed the frankness and passion with which they spoke and learned much from them. I am also grateful to Heribert Adam and Chris Saunders, who not only signed up as members of the summer school class but also read the lectures and commented most usefully on them.

But if the summer school played midwife to this text, its gestation was much longer and its progenitors more various. For the last four years I have benefited greatly from teaching an option on post-apartheid South Africa in the MSc in African Studies at the University of

Oxford. Each intake of students cast fresh light, raised different concerns and asked new questions. Also in the Centre for African Studies, William Beinart and Jonny Steinberg launched an informal discussion group on South Africa; these Tuesday roundtables have run for the past six terms, probing at aspects of contemporary South Africa, sharing insights from fieldwork and research, and providing an opportunity to disagree with one another in an atmosphere of intellectual generosity and collegiality.

I am very grateful to Russell Martin at Jacana, an unfailingly perceptive editor. My thanks go to a number of colleagues and friends who read and commented on chapter drafts: Heribert Adam, William Beinart, Sarah-Jane Cooper-Knock, Steven Friedman, Ronnie Kasrils, Uma Mesthrie, Jason Robinson, Jeff Rudin, Chris Saunders, Ben Turok. None read with a keener critical eye than Eve – and my gratitude to her is for that and much more.

Introduction
The presence of history

Democratic South Africa is only two decades old, but the years since 1994 have been eventful and testing. South Africa has boasted a progressive constitution, a global icon, a successful transition to democracy and modest economic growth. It has also sustained a devastating pandemic, persistent poverty, deepening inequality and levels of violence and crime that disfigure the body politic. In the first decade of democracy, South Africans were offered truth and reconciliation; they were rainbowed and renaissanced and two-nationed; and they saw a civil and seamless succession as Mbeki took over from Mandela. In the second decade – from 2004 until the present – citizens learned to live with load shedding, Julius Malema and delivery protests, were proud of their World Cup, but shocked by Marikana – and saw an uncivil and rancorous succession as Zuma replaced Mbeki.

This book does not offer a blow-by-blow history of South Africa since apartheid. Rather, it analyses selected political, social and economic developments since 1994;

and does so by asking some historians' questions about the period: questions about change and continuity, structure and agency, causes and consequences. It is not a history of the present moment but a study of the presence of history, of how the past permeates the present. Some years ago, I was struck by John Iliffe's assessment of the long-term effects of nineteenth-century conquest and colonial rule in Africa. 'As each colony became a specialised producer for the world market, it acquired an economic structure which often survived throughout the twentieth century,' he noted; African colonies approached independence within economic trajectories acquired before World War I.[1] And it was within these structures that the first generation of nationalist leaders – Nkrumah, Nyerere, Senghor and the rest – saw their heady and confident visions constrained by international commodity prices, demographic changes and other aspects of their colonial legacy.

So, too, for South Africa. The nineteenth century casts a long historical shadow. Frontier wars and colonial expansion, military defeat or negotiated subjugation of African polities; the discovery of diamonds and gold, their insatiable demand for labour, and the embedding of migrant labour – these were in effect the first rough scrawls of what became codified and legislated in the twentieth century as segregation and then apartheid; they provided the basic structures of white minority rule and mineral-led capitalist industrialisation. They fed directly into key developments of the twentieth century, profoundly shaping rural and urban South Africa.

The year 2013 saw the centenary of the 1913 Natives Land Act. The law was passed after a much longer history of dispossession and land loss, and the creation of territories recognised as the 'home' of conquered peoples, administered separately, and variously styled as 'reserves' and 'locations'. The 1913 Act codified several discriminatory practices established in the former colonies and Boer republics. It 'froze' land ownership into certain categories and barred Africans from acquiring any further property outside specified reserves. It also sought to outlaw various forms of tenancy on white farms. Perpetuating the reserves as the 'proper' home for Africans (and, later, installing traditional authorities as adjuncts to white rule) benefited the ruling class in two main ways. Firstly, it created a physical and social space in which to contain large numbers of black people at minimal cost. Secondly, as migrant labour became entrenched, the reserves became the main supply source of migrant workers, cheaper to employ than men with their families living in urban areas.

Yet for decades after 1913, African families continued to occupy ancestral lands, run their herds and grow crops on white-owned land. The real assault on share-croppers and labour tenants came later, especially in the 1950s and 1960s as farmers mechanised their production. The tractor and the combine harvester were key weapons of class struggle in the countryside. Hundreds of thousands of tenants were evicted. The Land Act loaded the scales, historically, in favour of capitalist agriculture. Once labour tenancy lost its rationale in the face of mechanised farming, those Africans who remained on the farms were poorly paid wage-earners. The anger and desperation of farm workers on strike in 2012, unable to afford basic foodstuffs, was a reminder of just how lastingly the 1913 Act and its consequences have condemned rural workers to the margins.

The face of South African cities is also deeply scarred by history. From the nineteenth century on, cities were the key arena for spatial segregation and social differentiation. The Natives Urban Areas Act of 1923 consolidated and extended existing practices, giving municipalities greater powers to enforce residential segregation and more control over movement. On this platform was constructed the vast apparatus of urban control under apartheid: cities deeply divided, movements controlled by pass laws, labour bureaux and forced removals. Here was the template of the all-too-familiar social geography of South African cities: white suburbs and factories served by dormitory townships. Here developed the mode of policing South Africa's urban spaces, from the impersonal to the intimate: from the routine demands for the *dompas* to the prurient midnight raids on servants' quarters (or *kayas*). In the 1980s, urban townships became the major base of organised resistance to the apartheid state – and the repertoire of protest developed then has been reprised over the past decade.

In the countryside as in cities, structures and behaviours made in the past press upon current policies and practices, posing urgent political questions, and constraining their answers. Let me cite one further instance of how the African National Congress (ANC) government operates upon terrain laid out in the nineteenth century, elaborated in the twentieth, and inescapably relevant in the twenty-first. Consider the rapid growth of the mining industry: how diggers and small operators were swept aside in Kimberley and Johannesburg, replaced by large mining houses; how these attracted direct foreign investment, created a cartel to protect profits, and welded into place a labour force with a skilled (white) artisan base and a massive, migrant (black) workforce. 'It is impossible to understand our present and its challenges without understanding this history,' Jeremy Cronin has written. 'What once propelled spectacular growth has shaped and distorted South Africa's economy and our broader social, political and spatial realities ever since. South Africa's economy is still excessively dependent on the export of unbeneficiated minerals. Our manufacturing sector, with exceptions, is weakly developed, as is the small and medium enterprise sector. The dominance of the mineral-energy-finance complex is hard-wired into our society.'[2] Cronin called his article 'How history haunts us'. He wrote it a few months before the Marikana massacre: migrant mine-workers in a protest over wages; over-zealous police defended by their political superiors – the ghosts of the past could not have taken more physical form.

Acknowledging the presence of history, then, is central to the chapters that follow. The argument is straightforward, but essential: thinking historically about the present means locating current developments (and future possibilities) not just since 1994 but within the longer term. It means identifying patterns of accumulation and exploitation that lasted for decades, so that economic structures and social relations have deep roots. South Africans sometimes seem to think that history began in 1994, or at least that the past ended then. Taking seriously the presence of history warns one against over-privileging the drama of 1994, significant though it was. None of the policies and ideological endeavours of the past twenty years began with a clean slate.

Phenomena usually described as 'post-apartheid' often have longer histories. Take three policy directions strongly identified with the ANC government. Firstly, a major outcome of the ANC's social policy has been a steep increase in welfare spending. South Africa now spends over 3% of GDP on pensions and grants, which go to over 18 million people. This is arguably the most significant redistribution of income achieved by the ANC, and the poorest of the poor are major beneficiaries. However, upon closer inspection, this shift was not actually pioneered by post-apartheid politicians. On the contrary: the movement towards greater social spending on black South Africans began over forty years ago. As apartheid certainties began to fray, the National Party (NP) increased the real value of the old age pension paid to Africans while that paid to whites declined quite rapidly. The pension paid to Africans in 1966 was only 13% of the value of a white pension; by 1980 it was 30%; and by 1993 all pensioners received the same amount. Of the total social spending (factoring in education, health and welfare) whites received more than half as late as 1975; but only about one-sixth by 1993. Thus the government elected in 1994 'inherited a budget that was already surprisingly redistributive'.[3] Using the fiscus as a means of redistribution has been accelerated by the ANC, but it continued a trajectory established during late apartheid.

Secondly, a central project of the ANC has been to encourage and foster the growth of a black middle class. There were two main thrusts towards achieving this. One was the use of state employment to reward and advance its followers. Exactly as the NP did for white-collar Afrikaners in the 1950s, the ANC has populated government departments and parastatals with its supporters. The other main way of creating a black middle class has been the use of Black Economic Empowerment to accelerate entry of black stakeholders into the boardrooms; to create and reward a 'patriotic bourgeoisie'. The emergence of black capitalists and professionals has been key to the ANC's social engineering since 1994; but, again, it did not begin from a standing start. Class formation among the African population was a powerful dynamic during the closing decades of apartheid, partly because there were ever larger numbers of better-educated black people, and partly as the outcome of policy. After the shock of 1976, attempts to create and co-opt a black elite were integral to President P.W. Botha's 'Total Strategy', and also urged by sectors of business such as the Urban Foundation. The number of Africans in 'middle class' occupations grew at more than 6% per annum between 1970 and 1987, from about 220,000 to 600,000.

Thirdly, there has been an explicit commitment by the ANC since taking power to creating mechanisms that afford organised labour and big business access to the state. Thus in 1995 it delivered a corporatist mechanism in the form of the National Economic and Development Labour Council (NEDLAC), consciously modelled on the social corporatism in European states. Alongside NEDLAC, there was of course also the formal alliance between the ANC, the Congress of South African Trade Unions (COSATU) and the South African Communist Party (SACP) created as long ago as 1992. And these developments produced a sizeable body of literature hailing a 'labour accord', 'social partnership' and 'co-determination', and discussing the leverage afforded to organised labour under an ANC government.[4] What much of this literature ignored or downplayed was the extent to which centralised bargaining and access to the apartheid state had been enjoyed by white labour and by big business for decades, in a form of quasi-corporatism that led fairly naturally to NEDLAC.[5]

It is also striking how rapidly the new independent trade unions, mainly representing black workers, entered similar relations in the 1980s. Each advance made by the unions 'drew them into increasingly powerful and institutionalised relationships with employers and ultimately the state'.[6] NEDLAC never became the negotiating forum that organised labour had hoped for, and within a few years had become a listless advisory council. COSATU continues its close but fractious alliance with the ANC (discussed in Chapter 2 below); but has failed 'to check the quickly maturing strategic alliance … being forged between the post-apartheid state and capital'.[7] COSATU's membership of the Tripartite Alliance is predicated on its acceptance (however uneasy and contested such acceptance is) of the high wage, high productivity, high profit and low employment growth path that the ANC has followed since the late 1990s.

These three cases – the expansion of social spending to benefit the poor; the hothouse growth of a black middle class; and the efforts by the ANC government and big business to keep labour on side as part of an 'insider' compromise – are important dynamics of post-apartheid South Africa. They also have strong continuities with processes in train before 1994. Change and continuity cohabit in post-apartheid South Africa. Understanding the shifts in their relationship is the challenge to the historian. Thinking historically about the present means locating ourselves – as individuals, as citizens – within our own histories and that of our society, thinking about what is historically imposed, and what is historically possible.

And that is the crux of thinking historically about the present: there is an inescapable tension between what is imposed and what remains possible. The classic statement of this dilemma was written 160 years ago, and has been quoted countless times; but it remains precise and compelling: 'Men make their own history, but they do not make it just as they please; they do not make it under circumstances chosen by themselves, but under circumstances directly encountered, given and transmitted from the past.'[8] Of course people have agency: they bring their experiences, energies, ideas and imaginations to bear on the present. They act individually and collectively, creatively and destructively – but they cannot wish a different present into being. Their agency is exercised within a particular present, at a specific time and place; people can only act within the constraints that constitute the Here and Now.

I try in this book to recognise both elements of this ineluctable condition: that forces and structures are 'given and transmitted from the past'; but also that historical changes and movements are brought about by people. Human beings (as individuals, or as clans, classes or other collectivities) are creatures *and* creators of history. Their actions, motives and capacities can shape and direct the society in which they live: but their social circumstances constrain and limit their actions and abilities. This is not historical determinism: I hope that this passage does not cause the same confusion that a short piece in the *Cape Times* elicited: 'is there an evil man lurking somewhere in the clouds called "Mr History" whom Bundy would like to punch on the nose?'[9] I am much more interested in ordinary people, on the ground and not in the clouds, and how they have shaped their lives since 1994 – and how their lives have been shaped by circumstances that they could not choose or control.

Taking structure and agency into account shapes the analyses that follow. It avoids simplistic or one-sided assessments of life under the Mandela, Mbeki and Zuma governments. It recognises real advances since 1994: the expansion of welfare provision to the poorest, a herculean house-building programme, a substantial fall in violent crime rates, and real gains in access to education at all levels. But it also identifies the limits and contradictions of such progress: the desolation of unemployment for millions; how 'RDP housing' replicated the geography of apartheid; how violence continues to menace everyday life; and how, in some respects, schooling has actually regressed since 1994. Each chapter asks: How much has changed since the demise of apartheid, and how much remains stubbornly the same? Should one celebrate a robust democracy now two decades old, or lament that political life is corroded by factionalism, greed and corruption? This Introduction has emphasised that the past permeates the present, complicating and constraining the politics of transition, so that genuine transformation has been short-changed.

1

The negotiated settlement
Brave new world or long shadow of the past?

How does one make sense of the negotiated settlement – the intricate series of encounters between the ANC and the apartheid government that began with the Groote Schuur Minute and culminated in an interim constitution and the election of April 1994? Various explanations are available. One is represented by Patti Waldmeir. Her *Anatomy of a Miracle* vividly reports the negotiated demise of apartheid. It was 'One of the most extraordinary tales of the twentieth century, in which a nation stepped through the looking glass and emerged as the mirror image of its former self'. Even more singularly, it was 'One of the great psychological transformations of the twentieth century ... a strange but wonderful tale of mutual liberation'. In her telling, F.W. de Klerk and Nelson Mandela were central to the miracle. 'History will surely claim these two men as its heroes ... compatriots, jointly devoted to ... their common fatherland.' They were both reasonable men, prepared to compromise; and in doing so they chose 'a future based on broadly common values'.[1]

Secondly, there is a view presented most effectively by Hermann Giliomee. He is not persuaded that negotiations were a triumph of reason, and he does not view De Klerk as heroic. The National Party (NP) leader was primarily a pragmatist, rather than a politician driven by principles. He was a tactician, not a strategist, guilty in the heat of negotiations of 'fundamental mistakes' and 'major errors'. Desperate to end economic sanctions, De Klerk rushed his fences and surrendered far more than he gained. This was partly because he 'lacked the ruthlessness that characterizes most great leaders in turbulent times ... He had no stomach for a show of force.' Giliomee is equally unimpressed by De Klerk's subsequent attempts to claim that by abolishing apartheid the NP was co-liberator of the country: this 'euphoria of self-congratulation could not last'. The Afrikaners 'had lost power, but were like King Lear', shorn of authority but expecting continued deference.[2]

Thirdly, there is a competing, but parallel, view: it holds that the African National Congress (ANC) was outmanoeuvred, duped, or that its leaders were guilty of betrayal. The ANC leadership in the early 1990s simply lacked the requisite 'progressive ideas and strategies' to counter neo-liberal ideas pushed by local businesses, the World Bank and the De Klerk regime; and a representative of this view warns darkly that we don't know to what extent Anglo American and other conglomerates used their propaganda and financial power 'to convince, coerce or co-opt ANC leaders'.[3] Alternatively, the leaders didn't need to be persuaded: the aspiration of the petit-bourgeois leadership was to join the bourgeoisie, to have access to state power and capital. In this dynamic, 'a small corps of oppositional politicians emerged to hijack the country's mass popular movements'.[4]

None of these positions is very helpful. All three rely heavily on the Great Man in History, providing personalised accounts which praise or blame Mandela or De Klerk. They dwell upon the motives and pronouncements of political leaders – but don't explain why negotiations took place; why they succeeded; or what their consequences were. This chapter examines the negotiated settlement by posing three questions. Firstly, why did the exiled ANC leadership and the NP government enter negotiations? Secondly, what was the *content* of the settlement: what political and economic arrangements did it bequeath to the Government of National Unity (GNU) that took office in 1994? Thirdly, how much did the settlement change, and how much did it leave intact? Was 1994 a crucial break with the past – or a moment illustrating how strong the continuities were, how tenacious the grip of the past?

Why did the NP and ANC enter negotiations?

"Why did the NP enter negotiations?" asked an SATV interviewer in December 1990: because it had 'run out of alternatives' was Foreign Minister Pik Botha's pithy response. F.W. de Klerk, looking back, agreed: by late 1989 it was very clear that 'the government's emphases had landed us in a dead-end street'. Even the hardliner Adriaan Vlok, the Minister of Law and Order, told a reporter in September 1989, 'Everybody ... realises that the status quo cannot continue.'[5] They were right. After four decades in power, the NP was in political, ideological and economic crisis. The apartheid project had run its course; and when ill health ended the petulant presidency of P.W. Botha, his successor and colleagues grasped an available nettle.

The crisis had long-term roots, exacerbated by more immediate pressures. One basic and inescapable source of pressure was demographic. In 1960 one in five South Africans was classified as white; by 1996, just over one in ten. In this time Africans rose from just over two-thirds of the population to over three-quarters. This demographic shift was sharpened by the fact that Africans were also more urbanised, schooled in far greater numbers, and more conscious of their subordination. A second deep-seated component of crisis was economic. For a quarter of a century, apartheid and growth coexisted. An economy based on white consumers, import substitution and cheap labour delivered prosperity for a generation: GDP grew by 5% a year from 1947 to 1974. But this growth path had deep structural weaknesses: a limited domestic market; a dependence on imported oil, technology and capital;

and an acute skills shortage. The South African economy never recovered from the international recession of the 1970s. Between 1975 and 1994 GDP growth averaged a meagre 1.6% and in the mid-1980s actually contracted. Fixed investment fell; external debt, inflation and unemployment rose.

Thirdly, apartheid never recovered, politically or ideologically, from the challenges of the 1970s. An assertive Black Consciousness, the mobilisation of black workers in trade unions, and of course the 1976 youth revolt which began in Soweto, defined new forms of political resistance to apartheid. Youth congresses and civics coalesced in the United Democratic Front (UDF) in 1983; trade unions linked struggles over wages and working conditions with community protests; the exiled ANC was a major beneficiary of post-Soweto politics – flooded with new recruits, winning international support, and able to infiltrate trained guerrillas from neighbouring states after the collapse of Portuguese colonialism in Angola and Mozambique. In these shoals, the Afrikaner nationalist project was holed and started shipping water. Soweto was central to an ideological retreat. An older insistence that apartheid was morally defensible was suddenly threadbare. Many Afrikaner intellectuals found themselves out of step with the NP; some became fiercely critical. While Vorster kept both *verkramptes* and *verligtes* in the NP, Botha could not. The 1982 split and Andries Treurnicht's formation of the Conservative Party wrote finis to Afrikaner unity.

If the NP government had lived with chronic crisis since the mid-1970s, the symptoms became acute between 1986 and 1989. A great rolling wave of protest led by the UDF was countered by successive states of emergency and unprecedented levels of repression. Economic growth ground to a halt. P.W. Botha failed to cross the Rubicon and the rand fell through the floor. Capital flowed out; there was an international credit squeeze; and tougher economic sanctions were approved. External pressures mounted as domestic weakness became more pronounced. In the election of September 1989, less than half of the white electorate voted NP, leaking support to the Conservative Party on its right and the Democratic Party on its left. Equally alarming was the realisation that the NP could no longer count upon the business community for support; leading capitalist interests (like those in the Consultative Business Movement) were already planning for a post-NP political dispensation. The NP entered negotiations because it had no viable alternatives.

The impulses propelling the ANC into negotiations arose partly from the domestic predicament of the NP government, but more decisively from the international context of the late 1980s. This impacted directly upon the fortunes of Umkhonto we Sizwe (MK), its armed wing. MK was formed by the ANC and SACP in 1961, and after the Rivonia arrests in 1963 a local sabotage campaign morphed into an externally based guerrilla army. Operating in exile, the ANC committed itself to prepare for guerrilla war – a task which proved to be enervating, complex and ultimately unsuccessful. By 1965, MK had some 500 highly trained soldiers, holed up in bases in Tanzania and Zambia, hundreds of kilometres from any South African border, desperate for action and dismayed by its absence. This remained the most intractable problem confronted by the exiled liberation movement.

Practical difficulties – such as distance, inhospitable terrain and superior enemy forces – were compounded by a strategic cul-de-sac. The ANC and SACP prioritised military action as a key element in the liberation struggle. They held that armed activity by a small MK force would detonate broader political revolt against the state – and for twenty years, the ANC relied on military exploits to develop political bases inside the country. Correspondingly, it neglected underground activism and semi-legal forms of struggle inside the country. This locked the exile movement into a fundamental dilemma: without an internal base, it was difficult to mount armed struggle; but without the demonstration effect of military combat, it was equally hard to build a domestic revolutionary base.

In the early 1970s, the ANC and SACP continued to invest resources in training and maintaining a guerrilla army, even as cadres aged and morale frayed. By 1973–4 fewer than 500 people were in ANC care, about two-thirds of whom were MK members, increasingly middle-aged and disillusioned. This ailing military outfit was rescued, reinvigorated, by the Soweto rising, its ranks swelled by thousands of militant new recruits. The independence of Angola and Mozambique provided fresh strategic options; new MK camps in Angola housed the bulk of its guerrillas. A strategic rethink in 1979 acknowledged that the ANC had underestimated internal resistance, failing to recognise the significance of the new trade unions and community structures. Henceforth the movement should concentrate on working inside the country, and MK operations should be aligned with community struggles. MK operations inside South Africa began in the late 1970s, relatively small-scale until dramatic attacks on SASOL, Koeberg and Voortrekkerhoogte in the early 1980s. MK attacks rose from about 55 in 1981 to a peak of 230 in 1986.

Despite these signs of renewed purpose, MK endured a crisis in the early 1980s with mutinies in its Angolan camps, met by brutal reprisals. The mutinies occurred because conditions in the camps were dreadful; rank-and-file soldiers resented the widening gulf between the life of officers and their own; and they chafed at the harsh discipline meted out by the ANC security department. Further pressure on MK was applied by the 1984 Nkomati Accord, which saw MK squeezed out of Mozambique, Lesotho and Swaziland, reducing its capacity to infiltrate guerrillas into South Africa. Such infiltration carried its own costs for MK, with very high levels of casualties, captures and desertions among those sent in.

A final, decisive pressure on MK came from the Soviet Union, historically its strongest backer. By 1986, Moscow signalled that it favoured political solutions to African conflicts, and that military aid would be scaled back. In 1988, the USSR and the USA brokered an accord signed by the South African, Cuban and Angolan governments. An immediate outcome was that MK must withdraw all personnel from its Angolan camps. An armed struggle relying on external support was no longer feasible. The military capacity of MK had been shredded – ironically, at the peak of its prestige. At no point in its history had MK ever held a serious prospect of defeating the SADF; by the late 1980s it struggled to sustain even limited guerrilla war. Yet through the urban uprising of the 1980s, MK's mystique intensified. Huge numbers of black youths made a cult of the guerrilla force, the toyi-toyi their rhythmic ritual. The 'central paradox that existed throughout the ANC's armed struggle' was the discrepancy between its actual military and material weaknesses and its immense symbolic strength.[6] By 1989, the ANC leadership was clearly aware of the gulf between militarist rhetoric and reality. In a famous gaffe in January 1990, the ANC secretary-general, Alfred Nzo, read to journalists a document intended for internal scrutiny: 'realistically we must admit that we do not have the capacity within our country to intensify the armed

29

struggle in any meaningful way.'

As the guerrilla project stalled, the ANC's exiled leaders, in parallel with Mandela in prison, began to explore the option of talking to the enemy. From 1985 onwards 'a faint whiff of negotiations was constantly in the air'.[7] That year Anglo American's Gavin Relly and a group of businessmen met Oliver Tambo, Thabo Mbeki and Chris Hani at Kenneth Kaunda's presidential game lodge in Zambia, the first of many political safaris. Emissaries scurried back and forth; meetings took place in London, in Lusaka, and in secret. The ANC met discreetly with British, Soviet, Japanese, Australian and US government officials. By 1988, Western powers broadly accepted that the ANC headed opposition to apartheid; that it was key to any negotiated outcome – and that it would relinquish its armed struggle. In March 1989 Mandela wrote directly to P.W. Botha: it was 'necessary in the national interest for the ANC and the government to meet urgently to negotiate an effective political settlement'. A year later followed De Klerk's landmark speech on 2 February 1990.

These interventions by the two leaders crystallised an emerging logic. The NP had suffered a debilitating decline; it had lost its certainties, much of its support, and its way. In exile, the ANC had clung to the limits of physical survival; recovered and regrouped; and by 1990 was swept by internal activism and international solidarity to the status of government-in-waiting. Decisions by party leaders reflected the balance of political and social forces in the late 1980s. After three years of swirling urban resistance, the government had imposed a shaky peace by *force majeure*. But while it remained militarily powerful, the state was politically weak. It retained the capacity to repress, but had lost the ability to persuade. For its part, the liberation movement headed by the ANC remained politically powerful, but militarily ineffectual. The state was unable to impose stability from above; opposition forces were unable to seize power from below. NP and ANC confronted one another in a 'hurting stalemate': the status quo was mutually damaging, but neither side could prevail. Both sides came to a reluctant recognition of the impasse.

What was delivered by the negotiated settlement?

There are a number of detailed accounts of the machinery of negotiations: the labyrinthine committees of CODESA (Convention for a Democratic South Africa) 1 and CODESA 2 and their successor, the Multi-Party Negotiations Process (MPNP); the late-night sessions, plenaries and working groups; and how deals were cut. These are not repeated here: the focus of this chapter is the outcome of the process, not its inputs.

At the outset, the broad positions of the ANC and NP were fairly clear. The ANC entered negotiations demanding universal suffrage, equal rights for all citizens and a strong legislature. It defined the future in terms of majority rule within a unitary state. This was a bargaining position buttressed by history, by international opinion and by the basic demographics of the country. The 1993 interim constitution confirmed it as the central political outcome.

The NP defined the future in terms of power-sharing, consociational democracy within a federal structure, and entrenched group rights. It entered negotiations convinced that it could avert simple majority rule as the outcome. De Klerk initially sought to construct a centre-right bloc, with the Inkatha Freedom Party (IFP) and the Afrikaner right, as counter-weight to the ANC. This strategy failed. From late 1992, although 26 parties were officially engaged in talks, negotiations were essentially bilateral, between the government and the ANC. Positions agreed by the two main parties were judged to have attained 'sufficient consensus'.

What did they agree? The interim constitution approved in December 1993 certainly favoured the ANC's initial positions: there would be a bill of rights; elections at all levels of government would be on the basis of one person, one vote; although nine provinces would exercise certain powers, substantive power would reside at the centre. The main political concessions made by the ANC were time-bound. A 'sunset clause' gave security of tenure to white civil servants; after the first election, all parties with 20 seats or more in the National Assembly would be represented within a Government of National Unity (GNU); and amnesty would be offered to individuals in the security forces in exchange for full disclosure of abuses of power.

That was the political outcome. It left unanswered the question of what socio-economic relations the new order would promote. Would majority rule mean redistribution from the few to the many? What development path would the new state pursue? How closely would it stick to international orthodoxy – or how far would it dare challenge it? Answers to these questions lay largely outside the negotiating chambers. The bill of rights included a right to property and the interim constitution provided for an independent Reserve Bank; but multi-party talks did not reveal the direction of economic policy in a democratic South Africa, or in whose interests a new order would govern.

Before 1990, the ANC paid surprisingly little attention to economic policies. It remained rhetorically committed to the Freedom Charter's promise to nationalise banks, mines and monopolies; a pledge repeated by Mandela, on the evening of his release from prison. But entry into negotiations meant that the ANC could no longer rely on slogans, but would have to consider policies, priorities and possibilities. With hindsight, it is clear that the movement's journey on this new terrain involved a dramatic change of direction, and a political retreat. In six short years the ANC's economic policy set off from a socialist platform, chugged briefly along a social democratic branch line, but ultimately steamed into Neo-liberal Central.

In 1990, the ANC held a conference in Harare and engaged substantially with economic policies for the first time. The discussion document that emerged was radical in tone but vague on details. It envisaged an interventionist state, emphasised the need for redistribution and restructuring, but avoided any mention of socialism. In 1992, the policy document *Ready to Govern*, adopted at the ANC national conference, distanced the movement further from radical readings of the Freedom Charter. It was silent on nationalisation, and specified that legal compliance and compensation should govern any transfer of property; it dropped an earlier promise to restructure the finance sector, and hailed the role of a 'dynamic private sector' in achieving growth.

These draft policies provoked a ferment of debate within the ANC, its Mass Democratic Movement support base, and its Alliance partners, the SACP and COSATU. When, in 1991, Trevor Manuel and Tito Mboweni headed the ANC's economic desk, there was a shift in register. ANC leaders now projected more moderate, business-friendly policies. A gap opened between their pragmatic repositioning and the views of grassroots activists calling for restructuring and redistribution. A third position was represented by COSATU. Uneasy at the ANC's direction of travel, and clear about its own commitment to economic transformation, it sought to bridge the gap. The unions pushed first for round-table talks about the economic future, with organised labour in one of the chairs. Denied an 'economic CODESA', COSATU opted instead for corporatist mechanisms, where business, labour and the state would negotiate and 'co-determine' policy. There was a flurry of papers championing a 'labour accord', 'social dialogue' or 'social partnership'. COSATU welcomed the National Economic Forum, launched in October 1992; but a year later the unions and ANC were pulling in opposite directions. COSATU again called for a summit on macroeconomic policy; the ANC opted instead for the Mopani Lodge meeting, with black business organisations, where the commitment to Black Economic Empowerment (BEE) was formalised.

Understanding the 'great economic debate' as a site of contestation within anti-apartheid forces[8] helps make sense of the fate of the MERG (Macroeconomic Research Group) Report. In 1991, the ANC commissioned a report compiled by a group of several dozen economists, mostly based overseas and all broadly ANC-aligned. The MERG report was published in December 1993. It was social democratic and neo-Keynesian: it recommended a relatively interventionist and regulatory role for the state; the economy would have 'a strong private sector interacting with a strong public sector'. Specifically, MERG recommended a two-phase growth plan. The first phase would see the state spend on housing, schools, roads and electrification, kick-starting growth and creating jobs. In phase two, private investors would jostle for opportunity in a growing economy. Nicoli Nattrass, a stringent critic of ANC economic policy, acknowledged that the MERG Report was 'by far the most comprehensive strategic document yet produced in South Africa on economic policy', its proposals 'carefully costed and situated in what appears to be a sound macroeconomic model'.[9]

The MERG report was a coherent progressive option. Its authors expected it to be debated and refined. But by the time it was delivered, it was already out of step with the ANC leadership's thinking, and was brusquely sidelined by the organisation which had commissioned it. The working relationship between the MERG leadership and the ANC's department of economic planning (DEP) had been fraught for a year. But more importantly, by the time MERG proposed an interventionist state driving growth through infrastructural spend, the ANC had abandoned the social democratic model in favour of an economic approach approved by the business community and by international agencies such as the World Bank and the International Monetary Fund (IMF). By the closing months of 1993, the ANC was part of a Transitional Executive Council (TEC) – and in November the TEC accepted a secret IMF loan of $850m. As part of its submission to the IMF, the TEC submitted a statement on future policies committing itself to a neo-liberal, export-oriented strategy. State spending would be constrained, budgets would be balanced, taxes would remain where they were. The IMF submission was in effect a curtain-raiser to GEAR.

The details of the IMF submission were not widely known at the time; but the curt rejection of the MERG Report alarmed the ANC's partners and many of its members. COSATU, in particular, tried to regain ground that it felt had been surrendered by the ANC. The trade union federation now sought to bind the ANC to a set of pre-election policy promises. Thus was born the Reconstruction and Development Programme (RDP), issued in February 1994, essentially a COSATU initiative. The RDP was always a hybrid policy document; more ambiguous in each successive version; pro-poor in its broad sweep; vague enough to give the newly elected government plenty of wriggle room; and politically weak enough that Jay Naidoo's cabinet post (with responsibility for implementing the RDP) would be peremptorily dumped in 1996.

The RDP was replaced in June 1996 without much finesse by the Growth, Employment and Redistribution (GEAR) programme. GEAR was unveiled by a truculent Manuel as 'non-negotiable', and defended by a prickly Mbeki: 'Call me a Thatcherite,' he challenged. Its basic tenets were fiscal conservatism, deficit reduction, deregulation and privatisation. Unlike MERG and the RDP, which advocated state spending, GEAR depended on the private sector to spearhead export-led growth and win foreign investor confidence. The ANC, heading a GNU, implemented a macroeconomic policy quite startlingly at variance with its point of departure a few years earlier.

Why did the ANC lurch from centre-left to centre-right on economic issues? Firstly, the ideological moment was crucial. The collapse of the Soviet Union was the major external factor, tearing loose the intellectual and ideological moorings of much of the exiled leadership and key domestic actors. Asked why the ANC dropped its calls for nationalisation, Trevor Manuel replied in 1995: 'the collapse of the Soviet Union, the destruction of the Berlin Wall broke the ... revolutionary romantic illusions of many. [It] ... shifted the debate very significantly.' So there was a loss of nerve, a failure to contest or even interrogate the message drummed by local business interests and international consultants. The ANC leadership became agitated at the state of the economy: GDP stagnant, investment falling and deficits rising. Trade and Industry Minister Alec Erwin wrote in 1996 that 'In 1990, this was an economy heading for a major train crash. It was stagnant, shedding employment, insular and characterised by conflict.'[10] Tellingly, his retrospective judgement was printed in the *African Communist* (house journal of the SACP) but had been delivered earlier as a speech to a *Business Day* banquet!

Secondly, there was 'a total disjuncture between the economic and political negotiations machinery of the ANC-led alliance'[11] – ANC heavy-weights at CODESA were ignorant or disdainful of debates between the

DEP and MERG, and unattentive to strains within the Alliance. Thirdly, the ANC was directly affected by external actors, local and international. Inside South Africa, business interests closed ranks and fought their corner. A powerful group of conglomerates lent its weight to influence a government-in-waiting: as many as 250 business forums and coalitions courted ANC elites. The scenario planning exercises headed by Nedcor and Old Mutual were disproportionately effective in shaping economic planning. At the same time, consultants from the World Bank, IMF and other agencies clogged hotel bookings and ANC diaries. Looking back, the World Bank congratulated itself: a programme of hosting ANC interns in Washington in the early 1990s had been 'influential at the country policy level' and in establishing personal links with the liberation movement.[12]

And so the ANC leadership drifted away from its base, abandoned a broadly supported policy in favour of economic transformation, and embraced those economic and social forces that had benefited from apartheid – and would benefit further from the post-apartheid dispensation. Negotiations on the interim constitution were formal, every session minuted, their details pored over, consensus hammered out. Alongside them took place a less formal series of interactions, fluid and ephemeral, which yielded convergence. These were discussions on the economy, between economic and political elites. Representatives of the corporate sector and core ANC leaders met frequently, attended the intoxicating scenario planning sessions, and arrived at a common narrative. During 1993 (writes Sampie Terreblanche) ANC luminaries and business leaders 'reached a hugely important elite compromise' that ruled out any left-of-centre economic policies.[13]

The 'elite compromise' on the economy was not formalised like the political agreements, but its basic elements can be identified fairly precisely. The central goals of the corporate sector were macroeconomic stability, the opening of the economy to international trade and finance, and an export-oriented growth path: the neo-liberal orthodoxy of the day. An ANC-aligned economist involved in implementing GEAR reflected a decade later that a key group of conglomerates in mining, finance and energy 'worked ceaselessly throughout the transition to ensure that the new government would create the kind of macro-economic stability that would facilitate the further globalisation of their activities'.[14] The ANC was won to this agenda, and in return secured a commitment from big business to accelerate the entry of black shareholders into boardrooms and directorates.

The argument may be briefly recapitulated. The white minority government and the national liberation movement went to the negotiating table in 1990 because neither could prevail over the other; both had run out of alternatives. Once at the table, the ANC privileged the political over the economic. It played to its strongest suit and won most of the tricks. But it was not the only game in town. There was another game, with chips priced in dollars, and with croupiers who were urbane and persuasive bankers and businessmen. In 1993, with its economic thinking in a state that might kindly be described as fluid, the ANC nestled up to the IMF; it jettisoned social democratic measures such as pro-poor state spending and progressive taxes. It agreed to leave the structures of production, ownership and income substantially intact. In return for endorsing the capitalist status quo, the ANC won an undertaking from business to proceed with what we now know as BEE.

In short, the negotiated settlement combined significant restructuring of the political sphere and broad continuity in the economic sphere. The negotiated outcome was not only a political compromise but also a class compromise. Politically, it advanced the interests of the black majority and curtailed the white minority's electoral dominance; socially, it protected the interests of capital at the cost of the working class and unemployed. At its most basic, the political settlement was fairly radical; the economic deal was relatively conservative.

This is not to suggest that there was a conspiracy concocted between the negotiators of the two parties. To accuse the ANC negotiators of having sold out their supporters is to mistake a loss of nerve for a loss of principle. Similarly, while there was undoubtedly a process of elite pacting under way, it does not follow that Cyril Ramaphosa, Mac Maharaj, Joe Slovo and the rest were seduced by the sophisticated representatives of capital and the World Bank, hijacked by PowerPoint presentations and the Montfleur scenarios, ideological innocents in an atmosphere of convivial patriotism.

Accusing the ANC negotiators of having sold out or been duped assumes that they started as economic radicals, with clear-cut left-wing positions. This assumption misreads the ANC of the early 1990s. A rhetorical radicalism, citing the Freedom Charter and invoking nationalisation, was entirely devoid of any theoretical subtlety or depth. In exile, a vocabulary committed to 'the liquidation of economic exploitation' and a 'national democratic revolution' as a staging post to socialism was provided by the SACP. But by 1990 senior SACP leaders were grappling with the question 'Has socialism failed?' rather than stiffening the spine of the ANC economic policy-makers. Slovo personified the Party's slide from old certainties. A month after Mandela's release he conceded that the market was a necessary mechanism in a modern economy. A year later, he told an interviewer that the Communist Party 'has rejected the prescription of nationalisation'. And in 1992 he posed the question: What room for compromises?[15] For the ANC leaders, left-wing economic positions had never been embedded and were easily shed. Ruefully, the SACP's Jeremy Cronin admitted in 1994 that 'real inroads have been made by capital into the ANC ... their arguments are more attractive and more persuasive to a wide range of ANC leadership than the counter-arguments that are less confident, less coherent.'[16]

The accommodation that took place was not conspiracy but convergence. Both sides of the agreement – far-reaching political change *and* essential continuity in social and economic structures – were the outcome of negotiations conducted at a particular time and place, and reflected the balance of forces, locally and globally. Context is key: the early 1990s saw the most triumphalist versions of capitalist orthodoxy, aka globalisation. The fall of the Berlin Wall had left only one system standing; it was the 'end of history'. The best bet for a new South Africa – argued the persuasive representatives of big business – was to join the winning side, to accept the Washington Consensus. It was a moment when the balance of forces was unfavourable to poor and marginalised citizens, when choices had shrunk, the range of options narrowed. For the elites, it made sense to act as they did.

It was not a one-sided deal. Big business and the ANC needed each other. The early 1990s were precarious years. Political violence peaked between 1991 and 1994; the economy was in dire straits; the NP had effectively abdicated. Business remained highly concentrated and economically powerful, but was tainted by 'racial capitalism', its historical association with apartheid. It required reinvention as multi-racial capitalism, and was willing to accommodate a democratic political order to win legitimacy. The ANC negotiators promised to provide a stable, democratic government – which could legitimate capitalism. This was the core of the dual settlement of 1994. Whites 'traded the racial state … for assurances on civil liberties, property, and economic policy'. The black majority – the disenfranchised poor – won the vote: they became full citizens. The ANC leadership 'superseded radicals in civil society', signed up to economic orthodoxy, and entered the political kingdom. The settlement delivered non-racial democracy and multi-racial capitalism.[17]

In April 1994, in election advertisements, the NP proclaimed, 'We have kept all our promises. We have got a Government of National Unity, which means that the political parties will share power.' This was wishful thinking. Within ten years its electoral support fell from 20% to 2%; by 2006 the NP ceased to exist. There are poignant echoes, too, in the ANC's campaign promises at that election. The strap-line of the party's campaign promised 'A better life for all. Working together for jobs, peace and freedom.' An advertisement pledged specifically: 'The ANC has a plan. We will immediately start a National Public Works Programme which will create 2.5 million jobs over the next ten years'. This was wishful thinking. Over the next ten years, 1.2 million jobs were lost. The NP's belief that it would share power, and the ANC's faith that a largely unchanged economic order could suddenly create jobs, look equally hollow, twenty years on. But their failed promises accurately reflect the implications of the negotiated settlement, which delivered sweeping political change and a striking level of socio-economic continuity.

Change and continuity since 1994

Negotiations delivered majority rule within a unitary state. Accordingly, since 1994, an entirely new political narrative has emerged: the ANC secure as the party of government within a dominant-party democracy. The ANC has been electorally invulnerable, retaining the support of black voters to an extraordinary degree. Another component of political transformation was the rapid decline and demise of the NP. It desperately rebranded itself as the New National Party (NNP) in 1998; but watching the NNP's final years – until its hapless dissolution into the back benches of the ANC – was like rubber-necking at a motorway pile-up. The political sphere changed dramatically. In terms of electoral outcomes and party politics, 1994 marked a sharp, drastic departure.

By comparison, social and economic relations and structures experienced no equivalent rupture, but displayed quite striking levels of continuity. Those who owned factories or firms before the elections in April 1994 continued to own them when the ANC-led government took office. Wealth – assets in property or shares or savings accounts – stayed in the same hands. The mining conglomerates, banks and finance houses which dominated the apartheid economy remained intact and dominated the post-apartheid economy. It was a relatively straightforward matter to repeal racially discriminatory laws and to approve a legal order based on civic equality. It would prove immeasurably more difficult to redistribute opportunity, or resources, or access to employment. The overwhelming majority of people continued after 1994 to live in the same neighbourhoods, go to the same schools, and have the same jobs – if they had jobs – as before.

This may seem a trite observation, a commonsense expression of the obvious: *of course* (it might be objected) social and economic conditions persisted; such things don't change overnight. But the point being made about social and economic continuity goes beyond the natural tendency for life to be lived according to existing patterns and rhythms. It also illustrates how difficult it was going to be for the ANC to effect the changes that its leaders and their followers wanted. Make no mistake: when the ANC took office in May 1994 it looked forward to a future in which the ravages of colonialism, segregation and apartheid had been repaired; in which people had jobs, and homes, and security – that 'better life for all' so fervently invoked. But the same politicians who became ministers and members of parliament in the new government were going to have to perform their duties on a stage with tight dimensions, limited roles and a script written in advance.

The Introduction argued that to understand post-apartheid South Africa one must pay heed to history and recognise the resilience of the past. Subsequent chapters examine different aspects of the two decades since the negotiated settlement. Chapter 2 assesses the record of the ANC in government, its electoral appeal, its relations with its Tripartite Alliance partners and its internal strains. Chapters 3 and 4 examine developments in local government and housing and in crime and policing as case studies of policy formulation and implementation. These and other arenas of government witnessed heroic levels of effort and initiatives – *and* utterly dismaying failures to bring about substantial, real change. Aspects of change and continuity are discussed in these chapters; here a brief overview is offered, a snapshot of what has taken place in terms of growth, wealth, poverty and inequality in the years since 1994.

The good news is that poverty has been somewhat reduced. The number of people living in absolute poverty has fallen. The proportion of the population living in absolute poverty – below a poverty line of R2060 per month for a family of four – fell from 56.9% to 51.7% between 1993 and 2008.[18] Mitigation of the effects of poverty has been achieved almost entirely through welfare spending. South Africa has become an unusually big social spender for a middle-income country: welfare spending amounted to R94 billion by 2010, or 3.5% of GDP. Numbers of those receiving pensions and grants have risen very rapidly: from 2.4 million in 1994 to 18 million by 2010. This has been one of the most dramatic interventions by successive ANC governments, and one of the most important forms of post-apartheid redistribution.

There are further encouraging data in the 2011 Census. Household income, averaged over the entire population and adjusted for inflation, increased by nearly 25% between 2001 and 2011. But averages, especially in a context of high inequality, can conceal as much as they reveal: many of the gains were concentrated in a wealthy stratum, an 'upper class' with household earnings of more than R10,000 per person per month. Between 1993 and 2008, this upper class increased its share of the national income from 17% to 32%, even though it includes only 1.3% of the total population.[19] Perhaps the most relevant data in the Census, with respect to improved living standards, is represented in access to basic services. In 2011, 73.4% of the population had access to piped water; 60% had flush toilets; and 85% used electricity for lighting.

The bad news is that millions of people – half the population – remain impoverished. Without the social welfare safety net, the level of absolute poverty would have risen. The major driver of poverty in South Africa remains a cruelly high unemployment rate. And there is even worse news, given expectations in 1994. Poverty may have been ameliorated since 1994, but inequality has actually risen. South Africa became a highly unequal society over many generations; but over the last twenty years the level of inequality has actually risen. Two statistical movements are clearly visible. Firstly, inter-racial inequality has flattened out: the share of total income earned by whites has declined, quite significantly: the share of total income earned by Africans has risen. Secondly, intra-racial inequality has increased: an African middle class has grown rapidly since 1994, accelerated by state employment, by movement into managerial and professional posts opened up by the end of apartheid, and by the hothouse growth of an entrepreneurial elite through BEE. In 2006, the Merrill Lynch World Wealth Report identified 5580 new dollar millionaires in South Africa produced in the previous year – the highest per capita rate of increase in the world.[20] In consequence, inequality within the African population is now as pronounced as within the population as a whole. There are over 250,000 Africans in that 'upper class' of high earners (from only 19,000 in 1993); and there are about 5.4 million Africans in a 'middle class' (which includes many blue-collar workers) with household incomes of between R1400 and R10,000 per person per month.

The evidence is unequivocal. Wealth in South Africa has been partly deracialised. Poverty remains strongly racialised, visited with particular severity upon Africans, at the bottom of the economic pecking order now as they were under apartheid. In 1993, Mike Morris wrote presciently, warning that 'Powerful forces are leading us towards a new Two Nations society, a 50% solution that will allow some South Africans to embrace opportunity and privilege, but banish the rest to the margins'.[21] A well-to-do multi-racial upper and middle class inhabits a different physical, social and ideological space from a dirt-poor black lumpen proletariat and army of the unemployed.

The evidence of how our history haunts our present is overwhelming. And if one moves from the brute material legacy of the past, and confronts what has been inherited in the realms of culture, behaviour and experience, the picture is no more comforting, the ghosts no less real. Arguably the single most intractable, most toxic presence of the past is how profoundly racialised South African society remains. The discriminatory divisions and hierarchies of apartheid translated into everyday experience and impacted on the psyche of all South Africans. The grammar of difference has enormously complicated the task of narrating a common nationhood.

Inherited structures of exploitation, poverty and inequality were going to be hugely difficult to unmake after 1994. The terms of the negotiated settlement made their reversal even more unlikely. Mandela's government was committed in advance to deregulation, privatisation and liberalisation of the South African economy. And for fifteen years (until the global recession of 2009) South African capitalism benefited from these promissory notes. The largest corporations globalised, restructured and listed overseas. There was a massive outflow of capital; concentration of ownership intensified and the fastest-growing sector was finance. The economy grew: at just under 3% a year until 2003, and then at a heady 5% from 2004 to 2008. But this success story took place in the global economy, and its benefits were not available for state action to reverse the tide of local history. The negotiated settlement equipped big business to strut its stuff on the global stage. It also limited the ANC's room for manoeuvre.

In order to balance its budgets, the ANC government ran down institutional capacity, leaving vast numbers of state positions vacant. In order to reduce its deficit, the government postponed spending on infrastructure. In order to win the fickle affections of foreign investors, the government took on the public sector unions. Public works, job creation and an industrial strategy to grow local manufacturing were non-starters.

The new South Africa has developed and dithered in the shadow of the old South Africa. A great novelist writing about another segregated society famously said, 'The past is never dead. It's not even past.'[22]

2

The ANC in government
Dilemmas of power

It is easy to imagine two accounts of the ANC in office which present diametrically opposed assessments. The first is a success story. Politically, the ANC replaced authoritarian minority rule with multi-party democracy, created a viable government and delivered stability and continuity. The ANC governs a democratic state in which individual rights and the rule of law are guaranteed, and which has an independent judiciary, free press and active civil society. Economically, the ANC inherited a crisis, but achieved fiscal stability and economic revival, ushering in the longest uninterrupted growth period since the 1960s. National debt and budget deficits were reduced. South Africans have benefited: middle-class incomes grew substantially; poorer South Africans benefited through a massive extension of services: numbers of formal dwellings, piped water and electricity have risen continuously and substantially. Internationally, the ANC rescued South Africa from pariah status and installed it as a respected regional power, punching above its weight in international forums and now a member of an influential grouping of emerging economies. By any reckoning, this account might conclude, the combination of political stability, economic growth and international profile is impressive.

But the second account is a study in failure. It insists that the ANC has lost its way as a party and as government. It has been racked by savage feuds, which led to Jacob Zuma's election as head of the party and the unconstitutional ousting of President Mbeki eight months later. The ANC remains riddled with factionalism. Old habits of secrecy, intolerance of criticism and hostility to the media persist, and elements within the ANC resent the constraints imposed by constitution and judiciary. As government, the ANC's reputation has been shredded by a combination of corruption and lack of capacity, leading to sustained protests by its own support base. Economically, the ANC has failed dismally in two areas. It has seen unemployment spiral to levels not reached even during the twilight years of apartheid; and so far from making an unequal society more equitable, it has actually allowed income and distribution to become more lopsided. The poorest 20% of the population currently receives 1.6% of national income. By any reckoning, this account might conclude, the combination of political drift, factionalism, corruption and social exclusion is depressing.

It is not that one of these narratives is right and

the other wrong. Both are artificial, highly selective and peremptorily one-sided. This chapter provides an account different from either: not by simply splicing them together, but by confronting ambiguities that they avoided and complicating their simplistic certainties.

Thabo Mbeki and the 'dramatic arc'

To think coherently about the ANC in power, it is useful to consider Thabo Mbeki. Placing him at the centre of a drama that runs from the mid-1980s to today helps chart the shifting contours of liberation movement-turned-government. Act I is set in exile: it is dominated by Prince Charming; adviser to Oliver Tambo, ever-present at meetings with Afrikaner politicians and opinion-makers, who were 'charmed and bedazzled by this brilliant, thoughtful, lucid man'.[1] Mbeki was in his forties, confident and charismatic, and, throughout the talks-about-talks and political preliminaries, very much the ANC's leading man – adept and subtle at the formal meeting, warm and winning with whisky glass and pipe in hand at the end of the day.

In Act II the Crown Prince worked his way centre-stage. In 1990 Mbeki returned to South Africa after 28 years in exile. He was involved in negotiations, although no longer as centrally as in the exile meetings. In 1991 the ANC held its national conference in Durban; two thousand delegates signalled strong leftist sympathies, rallying behind MK heroes Joe Slovo, Chris Hani and

Ronnie Kasrils, and UDF and COSATU 'inziles' Cyril Ramaphosa, Cheryl Carolus and Mosiuoa Lekota. But that outcome was reversed as the 1994 elections neared: Hani had been assassinated, and Ramaphosa sidelined, as 'the personnel, practices and conventions of the Lusaka ANC' triumphed, with Mbeki a natural beneficiary.[2] Mandela's first cabinet was a balancing act, and an awkward trade-off created two Vice-Presidents: De Klerk and Mbeki. By 1996, while Madiba gave himself to the tasks of nation-building and reconciliation, Mbeki was the hands-on driver of government. In 1997, at its Mafikeng conference, the ANC elected Mbeki as its president. The Crown Prince was now also Heir Apparent.

Act III saw the accession of the Philosopher King. In the 1999 election the ANC increased its vote to within a whisker of a two-thirds majority; Mbeki was sworn in as the country's President. His first term of office could hardly have been more contentious (or so it seemed until his second, uncompleted term) and has been extensively analysed.[3] Even the most summary account of those five years would include: ideas, visions and vendettas; modernising and moralising; state power vigorously applied and misapplied; and the destructive consequences of Mbeki's own personality and behaviour. Mbeki wrote many of his own speeches and a weekly newsletter: these were variously soaring, allusive, idealistic, repetitive, dogmatic and vindictive. His political philosophy melded grandiose ideas with technocratic pragmatism. The

African Renaissance hailed a new 'century of the African peoples'. Yet the means to this end were essentially World Bank nostrums – good governance, transparency and accountability – a mix pinpointed as 'Kwame Nkrumah meets Tony Blair'.[4] Politically, Mbeki centralised processes and structures: the executive was strengthened at the cost of parliament; policy and coordination functions were concentrated in the Presidency.

In the classic theory of the 'dramatic arc', Act III is the turning point: when affairs shift against the protagonist, often revealing his hidden weaknesses. Obeying this model, Mbeki's intolerance of dissent quickened: prickliness became paranoia. He arraigned critics, real and imagined. Cyril Ramaphosa, Tokyo Sexwale and Mathews Phosa were plotters; Pallo Jordan must withdraw criticisms of ZANU-PF; Jeremy Cronin must apologise for asking if the ANC was undergoing 'Zanufication' – and so on. Mbeki also became impaled on his own self-destructive stubbornness: what began as valid if heterodox questions about the aetiology of HIV/AIDS hardened into extremist denialism. He strenuously quashed inquiries into the arms deal, creating currents that would swirl for years to come. Then, in 2003, Mbeki rejigged the terms of reference of the Hefer Commission, seeking to discredit Deputy President Zuma and his confidant Mac Maharaj. This intervention, judged Maharaj's biographer, saw 'the revolution ... start eating its own – a time to settle old scores, personal and ideological'.[5] Bad blood circulated throughout the ANC; despite electoral triumph in 2004, with 69% of the poll, the party lurched into a protracted crisis.

Act IV in the dramatic arc is 'falling action', when conflict between protagonist and antagonist unravels. Mbeki precipitated this phase in June 2005, dismissing Zuma as the country's Vice-President because of his 'corrupt' relationship with Schabir Shaik. Zuma, however, remained deputy president of the ANC, and for nearly three years the ANC was embroiled in a rancorous and debilitating succession contest. (Mbeki sought to retain the ANC presidency, but to have his candidate – Phumzile Mlambo-Ngcuka – elected national president.) The ANC kept insisting that there *was* no leadership contest; that such matters were handled internally – but the race was on, the candidates running hard and barging at the bends. The two men were very different and their campaigns reflected this. Zuma's easy-going charm and empathy with people were his stock in trade: a consummate crowd-pleaser, dancing, belting out his trademark ditty *Umshini Wam*; pitching to different audiences in exactly the terms each wanted to hear. Mbeki's public forays and walkabouts were stilted, low-octane outings; his chosen terrain was not the party rally, but the committee room.

By 2007 the ANC was split into unforgiving binary camps, each feeding on rumour and malice. The intelligence agencies split on partisan lines: leaked files and hoax e-mails floated in sewers of intrigue and innuendo. Although largely conducted *sotto voce*, loyalties were being mobilised on ethnic lines. KwaZulu-Natal was Zuma's base; and his 'assiduous attention *to be seen* as being Zulu' was not happenstance 'but the cold calculation of a political poker player'.[6] Mandela had warned of the risk in appointing a Xhosa as his successor: Mbeki's cabinet after 2004 heedlessly heightened this risk.[7] But the crucial development in the 'unravelling' was that elements of the Tripartite Alliance marginalised by Mbeki now sought retribution. The SACP and COSATU leadership would use Zuma to punish Mbeki for his '1996 class project', replacing him with a leader whose humble origins, lack of formal education and populist style made him likely – they chose to believe – to pursue more left-wing policies. When Jacob Zuma cut into the three-metre-long cake at his 65th birthday party in April 2007, he was flanked by the beaming faces of Zwelinzima Vavi and Blade Nzimande, general secretaries of COSATU and the SACP respectively. The road to Polokwane had been signposted.

Act V delivered the dénouement. Mbeki and his inner ring were strangely unready for the circus that was the ANC's national conference at Polokwane. The pro-Zuma forces may have worn '100% Zulu Boy' T-shirts, but they were far from uniform. Zuma was backed by a loose coalition of 'disgruntled grassroots activists, trade unionists, socialists, unemployed youth, veteran guerrilla fighters, women's lobbies, supporters of causes ranging from the death penalty to virginity testing, black business tycoons, evangelicals, and the "walking wounded"[8] – those bruised by Mbeki's hostility to dissent. Conference proceedings were a carnival of revenge: songs, speeches and ballots rammed home the message. The Zuma slate swept into office with 60% of the vote, dominating the new National Executive Committee (NEC). In the months that followed, provincial and branch structures were subject to the same arithmetic, purged of Mbeki loyalists and stocked with Zuma zealots. Mbeki himself remained national President – until September 2008, when Judge Nicholson cleared Zuma of corruption charges and suggested that Mbeki had been party to an anti-Zuma conspiracy. The NEC held a hasty meeting and voted to 'recall' Mbeki: 'a *putsch* unconvincingly disguised as the democratic process at work.'[9]

Thabo Mbeki's rise and fall opens many windows on the ANC since 1994: its economic policies and their outcomes; links between voters and party; and tensions within the Tripartite Alliance. His presidency also prompts questions about the ANCs current trajectory, and whether it can find ways of addressing careerism, corruption and cronyism – tendencies which surfaced insistently under Mbeki, and which he repeatedly identified as inimical to the party he led.

Changing GEARs: From the RDP to the NDP

Other chapters explore policies in housing, policing and

education, but all these were located within an overall macroeconomic context. This section traces the ANC's approach to managing the economy, and how it was contested and modified over time. When the GNU – an ANC-led coalition – took office in 1994, it was involved in a complicated straddle. On the one hand, the ANC had already committed itself to fiscal orthodoxy, monetary controls, deregulation and a reduced role for the state. This was symbolically confirmed by retaining in office the NP Minister of Finance, Derek Keys. On the other hand, the ANC had campaigned on the Reconstruction and Development Programme, a sweepingly ambitious manifesto promising broad reforms for every sector of society. A week after the election, Mandela insisted that the RDP was 'the cornerstone, the foundation' of the new government. An RDP Fund would pay for RDP projects, and Jay Naidoo, until recently general secretary of COSATU, was appointed as minister responsible for driving RDP goals.

Today some ANC members view the RDP with a nostalgic 'what-might-have-been' fondness: if only the RDP had been retained, how different things would be. This is wishful thinking, and poor history. It overlooks the extent to which the RDP was compromised from the outset, cast in a conservative fiscal and monetary mould. It sought to help the poor, but not to affront big business. 'The programme to meet basic needs', explained Alec Erwin, the main RDP author, 'will in fact open new opportunities for the private sector.'[10] The RDP Fund was financed by 'restructuring' departmental budgets – by diverting existing line items, not by new expenditure – so that the RDP itself was sanctioned by fiscal prudence. A list of RDP promises kept during the ANC's first term is much shorter than a list of those broken.[11]

The RDP was unceremoniously replaced by the Growth, Employment and Redistribution (GEAR) programme in June 1996. Naidoo's ministry was closed. Although there were significant areas of overlap between the RDP and GEAR, there was something of a step change. GEAR was cast more explicitly in Washington Consensus terms; indeed, remarked Joel Netshitenzhe in 2004, it was 'a structural adjustment policy, self-imposed'; fiscal prudence was preferable to winding up 'begging bowl in hand' at the IMF and World Bank.[12] Widely supported by big business in South Africa, GEAR relied on a deregulated private sector to spearhead export-led growth and win foreign investor confidence. The period from 1996 to about 2001 saw the most rigorous application of GEAR policies. State-owned enterprises were privatised and outsourced; subsidies for farmers were withdrawn; and foreign exchange controls were swept away.

Proponents of GEAR held that macroeconomic stability would create growth. Judged on its own terms, the outcome was decidedly mixed. Stability was achieved; national debt, budget deficits, interest rates and inflation all decreased. But growth was negligible: by 2000 real per capita growth was lower than it had been in 1996; and the social consequences of neo-liberalism were harsh. Jobs were shed in the public sector, in mining, agriculture and manufacturing. An already vast army of the unemployed was swollen by a million new recruits during this first phase of GEAR.

ANC policy-makers rowed back. From 2001, a 'hard' version of GEAR gave way to a 'soft'. State spending on social welfare rose substantially to cushion the hardships of unemployment and poverty. A key policy document at the ANC national conference in 2002 called for a more effective state. 'We need a state that knows what it should be doing, how to do it and to do it well.' An effective state would improve service delivery, reduce crime, provide quality education, halt the spread of diseases – and so on. This signalled the Next Big Thing in the ANC's economic policy approach: the 'developmental state'. From 2004, the concept was ubiquitous; Manuel and Mbeki peppered their public utterances with the notion. It was modelled (roughly) on the success of East Asian economies; confident (rhetorically and ahistorically) of the South African state's capacity to drive growth and development.[13] During Mbeki's second term there were new emphases on infrastructural investment, upgrading public services and enhancing skills required by the economy.

Then Polokwane intervened. On Zuma's victory, claims rang out that the left had won; COSATU and the

SACP exchanged high-fives – 'a fundamental shift to the left in economic policy' was under way; 'important and fundamental paradigm shifts are occurring ... we are returning to the essence of the 1994 RDP'. These assertions overlooked the shifts that had already taken place under Mbeki. Zuma and his ministers, in the run-up to the 2009 election, celebrated the developmental state as though they had invented it. Had not the Polokwane conference passed a resolution on economic transformation committing the movement to 'build the strategic, organisational and technical capacities of the government with a view to a democratic developmental state'? Well, yes, it had; but in October 2008 Manuel reiterated the government's commitment to orthodox macroeconomic policy; Zuma told the Council on Foreign Relations in Washington that there would be no changes in policy; Kgalema Motlanthe, President between September 2008 and April 2009, stressed continuity and stability above all else.

Since 2009, under Zuma's presidency, the ANC's economic policy has largely pursued the path mapped during Mbeki's second term, making carefully calibrated shifts away from the fundamentalism of GEAR. These included symbolic measures, such as the appointments of Ebrahim Patel and Rob Davies to economic portfolios – rewards for COSATU and the SACP respectively – and more substantive measures such as progress towards a national health insurance scheme and the extension of the age limit for child support grants. Budget deficits were allowed to float upwards again – although not to an extent that alarmed business commentators. Both Davies and Patel have developed policies that aim at re-industrialisation and job creation; but neither of these approaches frames or directs government policy. That role is being played instead by the National Development Plan (NDP).

The NDP was delivered in August 2012. Authored by a commission of the great and good, chaired by Trevor Manuel, pilot of economic policy since 1996 – it was as predictable as its parentage would suggest. Intended to guide policy until 2030, it proceeds from some telling diagnoses of current failings to grandiloquent future goals. Its prescriptions are very familiar. It promises to 'eliminate poverty and reduce inequality by 2030', realising these goals 'by drawing on the energies of its people, growing an inclusive economy, building capabilities, enhancing the capacity of the state, and promoting leadership and partnerships'. (If this sounds vacuous, try some of the prose in the executive summary of the NDP: 'Now, in 2030, our story keeps growing as if spring is always with us. Once, we uttered the dream of a rainbow. Now we see it, living it. It does not curve over the sky. It is refracted in each one of us at home, in the community, in the city, and across the land … When we see it in the faces of our children, we know: there will always be, for us, a worthy future.')

The NDP seeks to steer South Africa towards a centrist version of social democracy-cum-market orthodoxy. The state will be attentive to the needs of its citizens, intervening to improve levels of education, health and welfare. However, change will be driven primarily by the private sector and not by state activism. Jobs will be created through 'faster economic growth' (achieved by increasing exports, not by public works or job creation schemes). The plan calls for a more flexible labour market, and takes a benign view of globalisation: 'increased flows of people, capital, ideas and technologies' have 'generally supported' development in middle-income countries. Although the NDP had been approved by cabinet previously, it was in December 2012, at Mangaung, that it was suddenly 'elevated to the centre of government policy'.[14] The conference hailed it as the best vehicle for the ANC to achieve its goal of 'uniting all South Africans'. Chance would be a fine thing! Instead, the NDP became a beacon of dissension within the ANC and its Alliance partners. COSATU leaders and unions have assailed the NDP as a neo-liberal assault on workers; in turn, Zuma supporters have fulminated against 'oppositionist' and 'populist' critiques.

Stepping back from the heated exchanges over the NDP, and viewing it within the longer trajectory of the ANC's macroeconomic policy, it is clear that the Plan breaks little new ground. It reflects the twin pressures on policy-makers: to redress the ravages of apartheid *and*

Table 1: Trends in voter participation, 1994–2009

	1994	1999	2004	2009
Estimated voting-age population (VAP)	22,709,152	22,589,369	27,436,819	29,956,957
Number of registered voters	no registration	18,172,751	20,674,926	23,181,997
VAP registered as %	no registration	80.4%	75.4%	77.4%
Turnout (total votes cast)	19,533,498	16,228,462	15,883,554	17,919,966
Turnout of registered voters %	no registration	89.3%	76.7%	77.3%
Turnout of VAP %	86.0%	71.8%	57.8%	59.8%
% votes for ANC	62.6%	66.4%	69.7%	65.9%
% VAP vote for ANC	53.8%	46.9%	39.6%	38.8%
% VAP vote for opposition parties	32.1%	23.7%	17.2%	20.1%
%VAP no vote	14%	28.2%	42.2%	40.2%

Note: Based on tables by Collette Schulz-Herzenberg; I am grateful for her permission to use this information here.

to placate the corporate conglomerates that dominate South Africa's economy. And so the NDP pays lip service to transformation and the interests of 'the people', but essentially seeks the approval of the market, at home and abroad. But given its constituency and its history, the ANC cannot acknowledge this, cannot defend its own policies for what they are: 'And so it is important for ANC leaders to say they are moving left when they are not.'[15] A leading scholar on the ANC concurs: considering the 'perplexing policy road' trodden by the movement for twenty years, she concluded that 'Members of its broad church, including the tripartite alliance, are kept content with neo-liberalism and revolution-speak operating side by side'.[16]

The ANC and the electorate

The relationship between the ANC and the voting public is striking. The party has won a consistently high level of support since the 1994 election. Over 60% of votes cast in each general election were for the ANC, at levels between just under 63%, to over 69% [see Table 1]. The ANC's strongest supporters are among the poorest South Africans. In Limpopo, Mpumalanga and the Eastern Cape, and in the larger townships, support for the ANC is in the 80% rather than the 60% range. How does one explain this constancy of support, especially from constituencies that remain poor and marginalised?

Firstly, real benefits have flowed to the ANC's main

electoral base, the African majority. For the very poorest, there has been much more expansive welfare provision, through pensions, child grants and disability grants. Even for families without wage-earners, livelihoods were stabilised, despair and deprivation cushioned. For the urban poor, there were benefits in the delivery of housing: the numbers living in formal dwellings, with piped water, electricity and flush toilets, have all risen continuously. A different type of redistribution saw the use of state employment to entrench a new, loyal petty bourgeoisie or salariat. As the NP did for Afrikaners, the ANC has populated government departments and parastatals with its supporters. Rapid class formation of this sort has an impact beyond its direct beneficiaries: 'an untold number of people have watched men and women whom they know rise from relative poverty to suburban home ownership in the space of a few years.' The message is clear: under the ANC, social mobility is possible, not in the abstract, but as lived reality.[17] Democracy paid dividends: and black voters invested their political capital in the ANC.

Yet voter loyalty does not rest solely upon tangible benefits and self-interest. It is also a statement of identity and belief. People vote for the ANC because they still see it as a vehicle of national liberation, victor over a hateful racist rule. This is what confers legitimacy and authenticity on the party for millions of South Africans. Writing in 2011, Susan Booysen observed that 'the basis of contemporary ANC power remains its liberation movement status', which creates a 'deep and forgiving bond' between ordinary people and political movement.[18] They see the party as more likely than any other to realise their dreams, to defend their interests. But how durable is the bond? How long can the virtuous glow of liberation shine? Is a point likely to arise when voters are more resentful of present failures than grateful for an idealised past?

Look again at the election statistics in Table 1. Firstly, there has been a general decline in electoral politics. While the proportion of eligible voters who have registered to vote has remained fairly stable, the turnout of registered voters has fallen from nearly 90% in 1999 to 77% in 2009. An even steeper decline shows up if one measures turn-out as a proportion of the voting age population (VAP): that is, including registered voters and those who have not registered. In 1994 a remarkable 86% of the VAP turned out and stood in those unforgettable queues. By 2004 and 2009, this level had fallen below 60%. And if one translates this into partisan support, it reveals that in 2009 just under 39% of the VAP voted for the ANC.

The 2009 election repays closer inspection. The ANC slightly increased its share of the total vote compared with 2004; but its proportion of the vote dropped in every province except KwaZulu-Natal. In Zuma's heartland, the vote swelled by a million votes, offsetting the ANC's loss of support in other provinces.

Nothing in these figures threatens the ANC's prospects of winning in 2014; yet voting patterns are more fluid, less predictable, than is generally supposed. Two factors should alarm those running the ANC's next campaign. Firstly, surveys indicate that the younger voters are less solid in their support for the ANC. Identification with the ANC is strongest among 'the '76 generation': older men and women, politicised decades ago. It is weakest among younger voters. South Africans under 25 are less likely to register as voters; and less partisan – less loyal to the ANC – when they do vote. Secondly, there seems to be a shift towards political pluralism, especially among 'younger, better-educated and more affluent African voters' – the conclusion arrived at by an analysis of data from a large survey conducted just before the 2009 polls.[19] The historical irony is unmistakable. One of the ANC's most fervent projects since 1994 has been to build and empower a black bourgeoisie. Now, as the younger generation of that class moves through better schools and universities and into better jobs, so their political preferences become more nuanced, less committed to the ANC.

Falling voter turn-out; declining support levels in eight provinces; a drift away by younger people – some of whom will simply not bother to vote, unless they are attracted by populist promises; others, their more affluent brothers and sisters, who will not necessarily vote as their parents did. These tendencies were already in play before the murder of Andries Tatane, before the

Marikana massacre. One cannot yet gauge the effect of such episodes on the core support of the ANC. But they have made it more difficult for the ANC to wrap itself in the mantle of liberation; to present itself as the protector of the powerless. The 'liberation dividend' will still count in 2014. The ANC will win that election, and probably the one after that. But its support will continue to decline. Susan Booysen quotes an unnamed ANC intellectual who told her in May 2011 that the party's decline 'is like an ocean wave rolling toward the coast … it will happen but we do not know the distance to the shore.'[20]

Alliance politics – and the politics of faction

In addition to being a political party and serving as government, the ANC has another identity, as a member of the Tripartite Alliance. In 1992, the ANC, SACP and COSATU entered a formal alliance. It was an important moment, as it marked the hegemony of the ANC in the anti-apartheid forces. The return of the exiled leadership, and the release of the Robben Islanders, saw ANC-friendly internal structures dissolve themselves in a display of symbolic solidarity. The UDF stood down as a separate structure, its leadership swallowed up into the ANC. Youth congresses, women's organisations and civic associations became part of the ANC Youth League, Women's League and ANC-affiliated SANCO respectively. There ensued an unplanned demobilisation of civil society. Popular desires and initiatives were brought into centralised and bureaucratic structures; the unruly and fiercely democratic practices of the 1980s lapsed. Foreign donors diverted their funding: countless NGOs were beached, and died. The set-back in the early 1990s to grass-roots initiatives and structures took a full decade to reverse.

Ever since its formation, the Triple Alliance has played an ambivalent political role. On the one hand, it symbolised nationalist victory: unionists and communists entered the political and ideological orbit of the national liberation movement. On the other hand, it has become a site of contestation, an interrogation of the nationalist message. Because no other party has come close to challenging the ANC at the ballot box, opposition over policy has been relocated to contests within the Alliance. Ever since 1994, COSATU and the SACP have seen themselves as the 'progressive' components of the Alliance, monitoring government's practices and policies from the left, pressing for more redistribution, for faster transformation. Mbeki's attempts to narrow the bounds of permissible dissent backfired, propelling COSATU and the SACP to replace him. For the ANC, the Alliance provides an arena where debate and disagreement are permitted, but tightly managed.

Since the 2009 election, tensions within and between the Alliance partners have intensified. One source of dissent is the issue of where authority in the Alliance resides. COSATU and the SACP have sporadically suggested that the Alliance should act as *the* political centre guiding government policy. But the ANC, especially secretary-general Gwede Mantashe, has made it clear that it will be the ANC, not the Alliance, calling the shots. Serious splits have arisen over specific policy issues, between the ANC and COSATU in particular. After the 2009 election, COSATU was dismayed to discover that Manuel's successor at the Treasury, Pravin Gordhan, had no intention of steering a different course. COSATU's public sector strike in August 2009 was ill received by the ANC; and relations were further tested by COSATU's opposition to the government on e-tolling, labour brokers and the Information Bill. Zuma echoed Mbeki when he lectured the left not to cross the line from criticism into opposition. In October 2010, things turned really nasty. COSATU, together with two high-profile NGOs, the Treatment Action Campaign and Section 27, convened a civil society conference. This evoked a hostile response from the ANC and the SACP and sparked an angry row-by-press-release, notable for pointed ad hominem attacks on Zwelinzima Vavi, COSATU's general secretary.

Vavi had emerged as the most senior Alliance leader warning that corruption and greed could derail the ANC. He assailed a 'predatory elite', a 'greedy criminal elite', which had created 'an oasis of opulence' for itself and was 'systematically robbing the poor'. Strong language: and it was not a single outburst. Since 2009, Vavi has been a consistent and incisive critic of the Zuma administration;

in December 2012 he was elected chair of a National Anti-Corruption Forum. This trajectory was always high-risk, given tensions within the Alliance; and after the consolidation of Zuma's power base at Mangaung, risk gave way to rupture. There ensued a concerted attack on Vavi by a loose coalition of COSATU leaders who also hold office in the SACP and support Zuma. Vavi is backed by individual unions, like NUMSA; but his crucial support resides within the broad membership of COSATU. At the time of writing, Vavi has been suspended; his longer-term fate is unknown: but the stakes are high, and those opposed to him seem willing to stop at little.

Under Zuma's presidency, COSATU and the SACP have pursued different strategies within the Alliance. The SACP opted to work within government, personified by the role of Nzimande, cabinet minister, SACP general secretary, and cheerleader-in-chief for Zuma. Currently, there are four ministers and four deputy ministers who are members of the SACP Central Committee: the SACP has in effect reverted to its practices in exile, embedding members in the ANC, and in return becoming 'a largely uncritical ally of the ANC ... and an opponent of those who would push it leftward'.[21] Grassroots SACP membership now stands at 150,000; Carol Paton suggests that it has 'become a power base from which to build a political career' and that since 2008 it has done 'amazingly well' in increasing its influence in government.[22]

COSATU is less promisingly positioned. Quite

apart from its internal power struggles, the trade union federation faces other acute problems. The social and political context which saw COSATU emerge in the 1980s has changed dramatically, even irreversibly. COSATU won its spurs fighting to improve wages and conditions for its members; it also played a crucial role in mass-based opposition to apartheid. Today, its leadership *and* its mass base are very different. Unskilled and semi-skilled workers made up 60% of COSATU membership in 1994; a decade later they composed 38%, replaced by skilled, supervisory and clerical workers (up from 35% to 60% over that decade). The blue-collar workforce that COSATU once represented so strongly is a shrinking social category. Industrial, manufacturing and mining unions have shed members as South Africa has de-industrialised. For two decades, COSATU could claim to speak on behalf of a broader working class. Today, its unions represent a minority of workers, and the federation cannot claim to speak for casual and informal sector workers, or the unemployed. Nor is COSATU immune to broader social ills. Corruption has stained the reputation of several unions; intolerance and violence have marred strikes; factionalism along political, ethnic and regional lines divides members from each other.[23]

There was speculation throughout Mbeki's presidency that COSATU might leave the Alliance to support or help form a left-wing political organisation to rival the ANC. This is unlikely in the short to medium term. Firstly, the ANC remains extremely popular with COSATU rank-and-file members. They identify strongly with the ANC as the figurehead of the liberation struggle. They freely criticise individual ANC leaders, and excoriate their failures; but continue to believe that the ANC *as an organisation* can be brought back on track, regenerated.[24] Secondly, COSATU's support for Zuma in the run-up to Polokwane effectively painted the federation into the Zuma corner. When COSATU held its 2012 congress just weeks after Marikana, it threw its weight behind Zuma's re-election at Mangaung.

The ANC is still the dominant political party. For many millions of South Africans, it still evokes the dream of 1994 and remains the vehicle of transformation. And despite tensions within the Alliance, the ANC retains the support of its two powerful partners. There is at the moment no political capacity outside the Alliance to challenge the ANC by capturing the support of the millions who have been left on the margins. The new social movements mounting 'service delivery' protests (see Chapter 3) do not constitute an effective challenge to the government. The ANC is discomforted by popular protests but not politically threatened by them.

Paradoxically, however, while the ANC remains entrenched in power, its vulnerability is as visible as its potency. The organisation (wrote Booysen in 2011) was 'simultaneously omnipotent *and* racked with internal and national governance weaknesses'. Recently, she has updated this assessment: the ANC by 2013 'had reached the point where its political power remained formidable but, by all available indicators, past its peak.'[25] The ANC is beset by various weaknesses, but three overlapping but distinct flaws are factionalism, corruption, and contradictions in the ANC's own social make-up.

When Mbeki and Zuma squared up in the succession contest, loyalty to each took factional form: positions polarised, rivalry became organised. At Polokwane, one faction triumphed – but the genie was out of the bottle. Under Zuma's presidency, the ANC became increasingly riven by polarisation and in-fighting. Factionalism became endemic. Factions could form around policies, around individuals (Julius Malema, Tokyo Sexwale, Kgalema Motlanthe), or most often they were shaped by issues of power, position and placement and the resources that these conferred. Rival groups competed at branch, regional and provincial levels, in government departments and in parastatals. Gwede Mantashe was blunt in his warning that 'infighting and destructive contestation' were a major threat to the ANC: 'The influence of money in our processes has the biggest potential to change the character of the movement from being people-centred ... to one where power is wielded by a narrow circle of those who own and/or control resources. This is at the centre of the resurgence of factionalism ... contestation is neither political nor ideological but driven by narrow interests.'[26]

The 'influence of money' expressed itself even more

luridly in corruption. The arms deal of 1998–9 poisoned the well on an industrial scale; its kickbacks and rigged deals have been replicated ever since in 'tenderpreneurship'; and public office has been used by individuals, covertly or brazenly, to loot the state run by their own party. To its credit, the ANC is alarmed by corruption and has tried to contain it. As early as December 1994 Mandela warned that 'a parasitic class in the ANC has emerged'; in 1999 he declared that the country's future depended on its resolve 'in dealing with the scourge of corruption', and the ANC invited business and civil society to join in the launch of an Anti-Corruption Forum. Mbeki, time and again, hectored his associates on the topic and introduced a 'code of conduct' oath intended to hold members to the straight and narrow. In 2007 Motlanthe conceded that corruption within the ANC was 'far worse than anyone imagines … Almost every project is conceived because it offers opportunities for certain people to make money.'

To its discredit, the ANC's hand-wringing has not translated into effective controls. There is broad agreement that the cancer of corruption has spread under Zuma's presidency. There has been massive media coverage of tender-rigging, abuse of privileges and perks, shady deals and phoney companies or trusts – not least as these stories have lapped insistently at the President and his family. By 2010, an astute commentator spoke of 'unanimity in the Union Buildings and parliament, in the ranks of business and trade unions, that corruption is the biggest obstacle to achieving South Africa's social and economic goals'.[27]

Factionalism permeates the ANC, inhibiting policy innovation and administrative competence. Corruption consumes resources; it also corrodes trust, dilutes legitimacy and alienates the electorate. In addition to these two challenges to the ANC's political dominance, Anthony Butler proposes that even 'greater challenges … have been generated by changes in the class character of the liberation movement itself'.[28] Black business interests, and those of the black middle class more broadly, now have sweeping influence within the ANC, and it becomes more difficult each year for the organisation to balance the interests of this elite with those of its mass membership, rural and urban poor alike.

At some point, these threats to the coherence and effectiveness of the party can no longer be contained. This might force the ANC into new policies, successfully reinventing itself; or the party might fragment, permitting the emergence of a rival body capable of winning a national election; or the moment could spill over into mass popular disaffection, in an ironic replay of the politics of ungovernability that hastened the end of NP rule. At present, the ANC seems incapable of creative renewal and, in terms of policies and practices, the likelihood is business as usual. Nor can one see on the horizon any new political party able to unseat the ANC at the ballot box: that prospect has been made less likely by the dismal failure of COPE to mount a real challenge. The third outcome was predicted by Moeletsi Mbeki. South Africa's 'Tunisia Day' would occur in about 2020, when China's minerals-intensive industrialisation phase will be concluded. China will cut back on mineral purchases, and an ANC government will have to cut back on the social grants which it uses to placate the black poor.[29]

How and why does the ANC find itself in its current predicament: in government, but with its power and credibility increasingly compromised? There are various ways of answering this. Firstly, a structural answer takes a step back from the details, and locates the ANC's embrace of conservative, market-oriented economic strategies within the surge of neo-liberal ideas in the early 1990s. It argues that this option drastically limited the room for manoeuvre, so that decisions taken in the 1990s imposed structural limits on the prospects for real changes in the country's social and economic relations. The ANC hitched its wagon to South African capitalism; and ever since then the major conglomerates have ridden shotgun, guarding their interests.

Secondly, a comparative approach assesses the ANC as a national liberation movement (NLM), and proceeds by identifying traits peculiar to NLMs. A magisterial study by Roger Southall argues persuasively that the liberation-movement-turned-government exhibited common features in Namibia, Zimbabwe and South Africa. Recognised for their role in national liberation struggles, the NLMs assumed the ability to speak for 'the people' (and therefore to paint its political rivals as somehow unpatriotic); they blurred the lines between party and state, using the former to allocate positions and contracts in the latter; and although they enjoyed genuine popular support at the outset, over time they grew distant from their constituency.[30]

Thirdly, there is an answer that involves political choices made by people: decent men and women, committed and serious politicians (as well as by others who were corrupt, greedy and arrogant). Imagine that the entire ANC parliamentary caucus had been gathered together in May 1994 and told something of what the future held: that struggle heroes would be guilty of corruption; that different ANC factions would use intelligence agencies to spy on each other, and resort to political murder as a weapon; that promoting the party faithful to government jobs would create incompetent and venal bureaucracies – and told also that unemployment would rise by 70% within a decade, that citizens would man the barricades in protest against delivery failures, or that the ANC would promote paramilitary policing responsible for the massacre of striking workers? Those ANC National Assembly members would surely have been horrified and incredulous: 'No, not us, not here.'

The imagined warning was not delivered in 1994 – but ever since, its details have spooled out. What is striking is how few members of that caucus, or their successors, spoke out as things went demonstrably wrong. Take the arms deal, the bribes, lies and cover-up: and as the story broke – what happened? In 2001 Andrew Feinstein, the senior ANC member of the parliamentary watchdog, resigned. Later that year, a sole ANC member, Pregs Govender, voted against the defence budget which paid for the deal. She resigned. Meanwhile, Tony Yengeni was the first casualty of the arms deal, found guilty of a relatively minor breach. Before serving four months of a four-year term, Yengeni was delivered to prison by a cavalcade of cheering ANC luminaries, including the speaker of the parliament he had lied to.

Or take the extraordinary saga of Mbeki's stance on HIV/AIDS. For two years not a single senior member of the ANC spoke out publicly, distancing themselves from the Mbeki–Manto line. Or recall the tragi-comedy of the vote on the Protection of State Information Bill, with Ben Turok – a real stalwart – trying to tiptoe out of the Assembly so as to avoid voting for the bill. One could go on, adding anecdotes or telling details: but the pattern is clear, and dismaying. Party loyalty overrode ethical judgement, time and again. From about 2006, some individuals voiced disquiet: among them Frene Ginwala, Ben Turok, Pallo Jordan, Kader Asmal, Jay Naidoo and Raymond Suttner; but they either did so in muted tones or 'once they were no longer dependent on the networks of ANC approval'.[31] The ANC has itself and its members partly to blame for the predicament in which it finds itself – and that of the country it governs.

South African cities
Sites of transformation and contestation

South African cities carry heavy historical baggage. They were the sites of the first major exercises in segregation in the nineteenth century. Under apartheid, they were the key arena for exclusion and social control, divided by Group Areas and Separate Amenities, policed by pass laws and permits. The physical and human geography of the country's cities was remade by apartheid. Take Cape Town: before 1950 it was the least segregated city in South Africa, its population patchwork a natural outcome of three centuries as a port city. But by 1980, after the destruction of District Six and the ethnic cleansing of Harfield, Claremont, Newlands, Simonstown and the rest, after the building of Mitchell's Plain and Khayelitsha, it was the most segregated South African city. Today Capetonians might consider that they live in post-apartheid Cape Town, but they actually still inhabit the urban geography of high apartheid. Cape Town, remarks Ivan Turok, 'remains one of the least altered cities in the world'. The destruction of District Six may have been the single most sweeping forced removal – more than half the population of the city centre evicted – but the cruelty was repeated in every city in the country: Sophiatown, Cato Manor, South End, Lady Selborne and North End are part of the litany.[1]

As the apartheid project ran into difficulties in the 1970s, it was in the cities that its defences were first breached, and then overrun. Especially after 1976, the NP government found it increasingly difficult to monitor or control urban movements, and its policies unravelled. Firstly, inner city districts like Hillbrow went 'grey' as new residents simply ignored Group Areas proscriptions. Secondly, informal settlements sprang up on the fringes of existing townships through the 1970s and 1980s: Crossroads (which won official recognition of its existence in 1976) was archetypal, as it 'survived, grew, and developed a defiant and uncontrolled culture' challenging the very premises of apartheid's urban regime.[2] Thirdly, in the aftermath of the Soweto rising, Urban Bantu Councils fell apart. An inescapable contradiction pressed upon the state: blacks, now a majority of the urban population, were still denied citizenship. These pressures translated by the mid-1980s into the township revolt. South Africa's cities became the major base of organised resistance to minority rule, and the repertoire of protest developed then has been dusted down and redeployed over the past decade.

The weight of this historical legacy is a useful index in assessing how much change has taken place since 1994: the transformation in how South African cities are governed, financed, planned and developed. It is also a measure of how profoundly shaped the urban terrain is by its past, and how deep-seated are the challenges facing those who work to remodel them. To start with the changes: it took less than a decade to carry out an extensive and impressive administrative restructuring. Local government was deracialised and rationalised. Old boundaries were redrawn; old agencies and structures were replaced; new electoral rolls drawn up; and the logic of one city, one tax-base was implemented. This shift was 'a very special experience' for those involved, changing institutions, ways of doing and ways of thinking quite profoundly. A single statistic reveals how sweepingly the system was overhauled and remade. Across the country the number of municipalities shrank from 843 to just 284. No fewer than 40 separate jurisdictions in the greater Durban area were melded into Ethekweni Metro by 2001; to form the Cape Town Metro, 33 existing authorities were dissolved.[3]

These changes saw city governance not just revised but reinvented; they amounted to a remarkable achievement, one of the most impressive programmes of transformation seen through by the new government. And these sweeping changes, by and large, worked, especially for the country's larger cities. These emerged with a new confidence born of greater stability and increased capacity. Compared with other emerging-market, middle-income countries, South Africa has cities that work reasonably well, are adequately run and operate as one tier of governance. However, this applies more specifically to the larger cities. There persists a remarkable level of inequality between municipalities. In 2004, a decade into transition, a government audit found that almost half of the municipalities – 126 of 284 – had 'little or no capacity'. Especially in the former Bantustans, there are towns stamped with signs of decay and dilapidation, their budgets drained and their human resources not up to the task. An account of some of these municipalities found that dysfunctional local government was conducted in an 'atmosphere of chaos and ineptitude … [and] a fog of lassitude, indifference and inertia hung all over'.[4] Even in the larger cities and metros, there is a series of unresolved tensions and policy dilemmas: the housing backlog, the deficit in the delivery of services, a concentration of new forms of urban poverty, hostility to foreigners, shortcomings in policing and a concomitant rise of vigilantism, to name but a few of the more obvious ones.

Against this background – of real but uneven transformation – this chapter considers some key features of the post-apartheid city: patterns and rates of urbanisation; housing policy since 1994; the spread of informal settlements and their significance; the persistence since 2004 of 'service delivery protests' and their characteristics; and, finally, some of the ways in which the physical and social fabric of city life is being shaped.

Urbanisation: demographics of change

There is a media cliché that South African cities are being flooded by rural people and foreigners in a pell-mell spate of urbanisation. The reality is rather different. Urban growth is very much governed by the availability of jobs and services and is very uneven. Thus the three Gauteng metros have seen quite rapid growth; the increase has been more modest in Cape Town and Durban, and has been very slow in East London, Port Elizabeth, Pietermaritzburg and Bloemfontein. These last four cities are growing more slowly than the overall rate of population growth in the country. Taking all nine metros into account, the increase since 1994 has actually been slower than for the period from 1946 to 1996. In smaller cities, the variance is even more extreme: Rustenburg and Nelspruit are growing fast; Klerksdorp, Welkom and Virginia actually shed population during the first post-apartheid decade. For the country as a whole, post-apartheid urbanisation has not been particularly rapid. The growth of the urban population, in any case, owes more to natural increase than to in-migration.[5]

A striking feature of urbanisation since 1994 is quite how unplanned and unregulated it has been. 'There has been no clear government position on the desirability of urbanization,' a 2006 study found, 'nor have government policies been based on clear spatial assumptions or arguments. The overriding impression is that government seemed to assume that the abolition of influx control would result in the gradual, but inevitable, permanent settlement of rural people in towns and cities. No new urbanisation policies would be required …'[6] This laissez-faire attitude certainly contributed to the somewhat haphazard grip that the ANC government had on the processes actually shaping the flows of people. Take the presence of foreigners, non-nationals, in South African cities. Any discussion of this issue must start by acknowledging how patchy and partial the data are: an overview of migration was blunt: 'No one knows how many international migrants are in South Africa, how long they have been there, how long they stay, or what they do while they are in the country.'[7] Such sketchy data are no basis for sensible policies on urbanisation or development – as was all too clear during the xenophobic attacks on foreign residents in 2008. Wits University researchers have suggested that the total of non-nationals is lower than popularly believed: perhaps 1.7 million in 2009, of whom 1 million were Zimbabwean. This makes non-nationals 4% of the total population: a much lower proportion than in the UK, USA, Ghana or the Ivory Coast.[8] Other estimates are much higher. In 2011, the Deputy Home Affairs Minister said that there might be as many as 10 million refugees in the country. We know that a large majority of non-national migrants move to the metros, where many of them encounter hostility and xenophobia in various degrees.

As far as internal migration is concerned, one of the most significant demographic patterns since 1994 has been the displacement of people from farms, mainly white-owned farms. Between 1994 and 2004 some 2.4 million people moved off these farms. Most of them moved into small towns. When they have moved into large cities, they are typically unskilled work-seekers, living in backyard shacks or in informal settlements.[9] Although this chapter focuses on cities, it is worth noting how little the rural poor have benefited from land reform in post-apartheid South Africa. Land reform has not provided a viable alternative to urban migration; has not created new livelihoods; and certainly has not slowed the drift of people into urban areas. Bill Freund comments: 'Surely, by far the most important aspect of land reform policy ought to be the systematic making available of land for an incoming population through expansion on the edges of the city ... but there is nothing of the kind.'[10]

Migration into the cities is driven by a desire for jobs and for services. By 2004, 4.9 million people had jobs in the nine metros: this was over 50% of the total working population in the country. However, these same cities represent the greatest relative concentration of poverty in the country. The nine metros contained 44% of South Africa's unemployed population: over a million people joined unemployment queues in the cities between 1996 and 2001. They were also home to 34% of all people living in informal housing or shacks.[11] Statistics like these hammer home the point that what happens in South Africa's cities lies at the heart of achieving a vision of a productive, democratic and non-racial society.

Housing policy since 1994

Post-apartheid housing policy is a complex and instructive story. It tells, firstly, of the drive and desire by the ANC to make a difference, to improve the lives of the poor. One of the most memorable campaign promises in 1994 was the ANC's commitment to building a million new homes in five years – which it achieved. Today, over 2.25 million 'housing units' have been provided: 10 million South Africans have been rehoused. By international comparative standards, this is a remarkable achievement, both in its pace and its scale, and for the fact that households in RDP houses have security of tenure. The 2011 Census revealed that 77.6% of all South Africans now live in formal dwellings. The delivery of housing and related services – electricity, water, sanitation – was crucial in winning legitimacy for the new state in the eyes of its supporters. It provided beneficiaries with access to basic services, security of tenure, and shelter. If 'transformation' as a concept has worn thin with over-use, in housing it retains its currency. But the story of housing policy since 1994 also reveals the gap between good intentions and unintended consequences; and illustrates graphically the limits of policy, the piecemeal and incomplete nature of transformation. The story begins with the negotiated settlement; specifically the deal brokered in 1993 at the National Housing Forum, where the ANC reached an agreement with business interests, represented by the Urban Foundation. The private sector pushed for an individual site-and-service model, made possible by a capital subsidy. The ANC, supported by civics and trade unions, initially sought a state-built rental model. The final compromise saw a state-built 'starter house' added onto the site-and-service model.[12]

Thus was born the 'RDP house', as it quickly became known, 'whether in irony or hope'.[13] For each housing unit, the state made a once-off contribution, purchasing the land, granting tenure to a means-tested family – either as a site or more commonly with a building of 30 square metres. The original expectation was that households would over time consolidate or add onto the starter home. This model lent itself to a target-driven programme of delivery: identical structures, one size fits all, on modest plots, on land that could be cheaply acquired, built through private developers. The emphasis on meeting targets and the subsidy mechanism 'directly undermined the urban integration policy' and exacerbated the tendency to locate housing projects on cheaper, peripheral land.[14] So RDP houses spooled out as RDP townships, often built on land previously bought or zoned for township development under apartheid, usually on the periphery of existing townships. The Housing White Paper in 1994 imagined that the scheme would do more than just build houses, but would deliver 'viable, integrated settlements where households would have convenient access to opportunities, infrastructure and services'. This did not happen. RDP townships, almost without exception, tend to be highly inadequate environments, with stunted facilities, rather than functional and properly resourced neighbourhoods. The houses themselves soon won a reputation for shoddy quality, for being poorly served by public transport, and for allowing no privacy or dignity to their inhabitants.[15]

Township dwellers who grumbled that 'Mandela's houses are smaller than Verwoerd's houses'[16] were making a valid point about the RDP housing success story. For the first ten years of ANC government, progress on housing was assumed to be a quantitative question: How many units had been delivered? Had targets been met? In the rush to build more and more small houses, 'it was forgotten that at the heights of its power the apartheid state had been one of the largest builders of state housing in the world' and that a properly post-apartheid approach should have considered the quality of houses built, their location and their access to affordable transport and facilities.[17] The herculean programme of house-building by the ANC has replicated and reinforced the spatial logic of apartheid, increasingly recognised by government. In

2004 Cape Town's planners lamented that their policies 'have simply and continuously reinforced historical investment patterns ... As the City has grown outwards it has become increasingly inaccessible, inequitable and inconvenient for the majority of the people.' Turok cites a 'variety of government reports and speeches' acknowledging how little has been achieved to transform urban life: succinctly, the National Development Plan in 2012 found that 'The apartheid spatial divide continues to dominate the landscape'.[18]

Nobody has written more eloquently about this irony – or should that be tragedy? – than Njabulo Ndebele. Here is a sample of his disquiet at the 'resilience of the inherited apartheid landscape'. 'For a people so extensively traumatised and anguished by settlements created for their dehumanisation, newly enfranchised South Africans have displayed an exasperating lack of urgency in their commitment to changing these conditions in radical ways. The townships, as these settlements are popularly known, are dormitory enclaves ... Dormitory enclaves are by definition built to export their energies ... Dormitory settlements are minimally administered enclaves lacking in form all institutional complexity. This is because the span of allowable social interest is limited to basic housing, under-resourced schooling, limited entertainment, limited formal medical facilities, limited shopping and trading facilities, extensive religious participation, high birthrates, and a network of transportation to export labour out of the dormitories. This basic conception of township settlements still remains fundamentally intact fifteen years after liberation and after decades of conditioning black people's expectations of human settlements. Dormitory settlements were not designed to stimulate the social imagination. Consequently, post-apartheid provision of housing has not produced bold models that represent alternative conceptualisations of settlements. The statistically successful provision of houses has not extended the horizons of social imagination. When we built houses, we forgot that the building of houses should have been more about building communities.'[19]

The ANC chafed under criticisms of the RDP housing project, and, after a decade in power, it seemed that a major overhaul in housing policy might ensue. President Mbeki, in his State of the Nation address (May 2004), promised that a plan would go to cabinet, within months, to address persistent poverty and urban infrastructure. In September of that year, the new Minister of Housing, Lindiwe Sisulu, won cabinet approval for a policy document called *Breaking New Ground*. The document was partly a response to Mbeki's insistence on the need for poverty alleviation, and partly the product of NGO and academic critiques of existing policy. It embraced the notion of 'sustainable human development'; proposed that new commercial developments would be permitted only if they provided 20% low-income units; and sought to change the subsidy mechanism so that in future houses would be built on well-located land. It also contained important – if ambiguous – provisions with respect to informal settlements: these are described in the next section.

Informal settlements

Informal settlements have been a feature of cities in developing countries for half a century. As cities have expanded, so have informal settlements – *favelas*, *barrios*, shack cities, slums, shanty-towns, squatter camps. The United Nations estimates that one billion people live in informal housing. In these areas, poor people survive, partly through unskilled formal sector jobs, but often in the informal sector. They turn to low-productivity activities, eking out a living on the edges of cities and at the margins of the urban economy. They recycle waste, collect garbage, scavenge for saleable items, set up tiny vending stalls; they cut hair, fix shoes, patch clothes – a ceaseless struggle for survival. Life in informal settlements may be tough – is tough – but it provides a way of accessing shelter, develops social networks, and brings people nearer jobs, transport routes and schools. One should not romanticise informal settlement as a form of heroism; but, equally, one must recognise that informality is a coherent strategy for winning a livelihood. Informal settlements are sites of resilience and innovation; the people who build shack-homes there are creating their own space in the city, developing their own forms of collective action and neighbourliness; overcoming a series of hurdles in order to establish a connection with city life.[20]

Informal settlements in South African cities tend not to be on inner-city sites, but alongside and within existing townships, or on vacant land, or land alongside major roads or railway lines. There are currently 2700 urban and peri-urban informal settlements in South Africa. To illustrate this at city level, consider Cape Town: at last official count, 243 separate informal settlements, comprising about 110,000 shacks, housed 22% of greater Cape Town's 3 million citizens. Many of them are relatively small, opportunistic peopling of unused land. Some of them are probably known to all readers of the *Cape Times* – Joe Slovo, Chris Hani Camp, Brown's Farm – but there is also a hidden geography, settlements like Malawi, Spandau, Westminster, Kosovo, Bonneytown Bush, Pook se Bos, Piet se Bos, Doornbach, Skandaalkamp and Table View tipsite. They vary, but have key features in common: they are tightly packed, densely inhabited; their residents have no security of tenure. Residents tend to be less well educated and less healthy than the population at large. They are keen to improve their lives, and believe that having a toehold in the city is the first step to doing this.

This is how Thandi Khambule, a young domestic worker, living in a shack settlement in a Durban suburb, explained it in 2007: 'For government this is an informal settlement but for the people who stay here it is formal.

We take our lives and our place very seriously. Yes, it is not formal in the way that the buildings are not formal and need to be made formal and in the way that we need toilets and electricity – in that way, it must be made formal. But it is wrong to say that it is informal as if it doesn't matter, as if we don't care. The thing is that if you are staying in the shacks you have got the hope that things will get better. If you are staying in Underberg [where she came from] you won't have any hope. If they take you to a rural house in a place like Verulam [where she was due to be relocated] you won't have any hope. Here the people have the hope.'[21]

Policy towards informal settlement, across the developing world, has taken various forms. At one pole is *in situ* upgrading: this begins by working with a given shack community, recognising its residents' rights to live in the city, granting security of tenure, and then working to upgrade the settlement, with community representatives involved in the process. Upgrading involves the provision of services, greater security and better prospects, but not necessarily the provision of formal housing. At the other pole is hostility to the presence of informal settlements, and a commitment to their clearance or eradication. The 2004 policy of the South African government, *Breaking New Ground*, seemed to embrace support for upgrading of settlements; it declared a shift from 'conflict and neglect' to the integration of informal settlements 'into the broader urban fabric to overcome spatial, social and economic exclusion' through 'a phased *in-situ* upgrading approach'. However, just as the policy was launched, there was a contradictory enthusiasm for slum clearance, for the eradication of existing shack settlements. The ink was barely dry on *Breaking New Ground* when Housing Minister Lindiwe Sisulu announced that she intended to move 'towards a shack-free society'. She went on: 'The Premier of Gauteng has fired the first salvo in our war against shacks. His bold assertion that informal settlements in his province will have been eradicated in ten years is the best news that I have heard in my tenure as Minister.'

KwaZulu-Natal followed suit, promising to eradicate slums in the province by 2010, and then upped the ante by rushing through an Elimination and Prevention of Re-emergence of Slums Act. To the consternation of many, the KZN Slums Act resounded with apartheid echoes: like the infamous Prevention of Illegal Squatting Act of 1951, it criminalised land invasions; exactly as the NP had done, it authorised municipalities to remove squatters and to relocate them in 'transit areas'. At Polokwane, in 2007, the ANC's national conference resolved to extend KZN's Slums Act into national policy. Since then, provincial governments have tended to identify shack settlements as the fundamental problem, rather than seeing inadequate housing as the fundamental problem. This fails to acknowledge that, in the absence of other viable options, shacks are often the only way of accessing the city and of establishing a household. And if the shack settlement is the problem and must be eradicated, what are the policy tools available? Why, tighter control over urban movements; the creation of transit camps or temporary relocation areas (unlovely areas dubbed *amatins*); and the physical destruction of homes – a toolkit familiar from the apartheid era.

The 'slum eradication' policy stance was hotly contested, most notably by the shack-dwellers' movement Abahlali baseMjondolo, based in Durban. Abahlali denounced the KZN Slums Act in memorable terms: 'Poor people must be allowed to stay in the cities. We need upgrades and not relocations. It is the Slums Act that must go. It is evictions that must go. It is the Land Invasion Unit and the Red Ants [hired security guards] that must go. It is the hatred of the poor that must go. It is the rule of money over the lives of people that must go.'

Abahlali took the Act to court; and eventually in October 2009 the Constitutional Court struck down a central section of the Slums Act, rendering it inoperable. Then in 2010 there was an unexpected policy lurch towards on-site regrading, when President Zuma announced that 'well-located informal settlements' would be upgraded, so as to benefit 400,000 households. Three years later, the Human Settlements Department (as the Housing Department became in 2009) remains ambivalent in this regard. On the one hand, the National Housing Code provides for the funding to municipalities so that they can undertake *in situ* upgrading. On the other hand, most municipalities remain hostile to 'illegal' settlements and what are dubbed land invasions, and they resort to strong-arm tactics to limit or prevent informal settlement from taking place.[22]

Service delivery protests and 'new social movements'

There is a strong link between informal settlements and the wave of local protests that have been such a persistent feature of urban life since 2004. In the year from March 2004 to the end of February 2005, a startled government learned that there had been 881 'illegal' protests and over 1500 'legal' ones (that is, where official permission had been sought and granted). Such protest action became a distinctive feature of political life during Mbeki's second term in office, and increased in volume after his removal. According to official police 'crowd management' statistics, the three years 2009/10, 2010/2011 and 2011/2012 saw just over 32,500 episodes of protest, of which 3072 were characterised as 'unrest'. By any comparative standards, this is an extraordinary display of grass-roots disaffection. Protests took place in most of the major cities, but also in smaller towns and in semi-urban areas. Peter Alexander has characterised the phenomenon as 'a massive movement of militant local political protests' which in some cases reached insurrectionary proportions so that 'it is reasonable to describe the phenomenon as a *rebellion of the poor*'.[23] Since his overview, such protest actions have attracted incisive analysis and it is possible to make some broad generalisations about them:

- Most of the protests involved residents of informal settlements, while others emanated from the poorer sections of formal townships. They varied in scale, duration and intensity, but drew upon a familiar repertoire of protest: mass meetings, memoranda and marches; stay-aways and boycotts; blocked streets behind barricades of burning tyres; attacks on buildings and on unpopular office-holders.
- Calling them 'service delivery protests' conceals as much as it reveals. While they often drew attention to failed municipal services – around housing, water, sanitation – their anger was broader than this. They also targeted instances of corruption and local favouritism, attacked specific councillors or officers, protested against prices and fees; they might express hostility to police or resentment of foreigners.
- Although much scholarly attention has been paid to 'new social movements'* (NSMs) within urban protest, this overstates their importance. Some NSMs have become players on the broader

---

* Defined as 'politically and/or socially directed collectives ... focused on changing one or more elements of the social, political and economic system'.

political stage: the Anti-Privatisation Forum, the Landless People's Movement, and Abahlali baseMjondolo; but the great majority are short-lived and less organised. Steven Friedman convincingly argues that NSMs 'have played at best a marginal role' in the ubiquitous protests.[24] A study of social protest in Durban, based on three years of media coverage, conveys an astonishing sense of just how various and diverse such actions were. The most common protesters were local residents, fleetingly organised; other actors included NGOs, university staff and students, local traders, ratepayer associations, bus drivers and commuters, environmental activists, members of a dozen trade unions – and many others. The South African Unemployed People's Movement protested in two foodstores, staging not only a sit-in but an eat-in; 'Umlazi Occupy' protesters pitched camp outside their ward councillor's office and remained for a month.[25]

- A striking feature of this wave of municipal activism is its localism. The protests are almost always geographically and politically separate from each other; they have no common political programmes or ideological platforms. In two suggestive phrases, these protests are 'movement beyond movements', taking place largely outside the scope of NSMs; they are 'unstoppable yet apparently unlinkable', given the weakness of social movements and the lack of strategic coherence.[26] The corollary of their localism is how little traction, within such protests, organised labour has. Although the trade unions remain the largest organised interest in South Africa, they have 'little or no presence among the growing number of poor people outside the formal economy'. Two conclusions may be drawn: that currently COSATU has placed most of its eggs in the Alliance basket and is unlikely to forge effective links with the municipal protests; and that until such an alliance is possible, 'it is unlikely that an effective movement for redistribution will emerge'.[27]

The shaping of the cities

How are South African cities being shaped, physically and socially, as the twenty-first century gathers pace? They will grow: urban dwellers are expected to increase from 62% to 71% of the total population by 2030, adding a further 8 million city residents. Physically, cities will continue to expand in essentially familiar ways. State-built housing for the urban poor will still be located on cheap land on the urban fringe, far from the city centre. Property developers and the construction industry will focus on high-profit ventures: expensive new housing for the well-off, either in existing suburbs or in new suburbs made possible by urban sprawl along excellent highways. Affluent suburbanites will shop in purpose-built malls, easily reached by those with cars, and virtually inaccessible to public transport. The love affair between the suburbs and the motor car remains intense, and the new highways shuttle people between separate spheres of work, leisure and home. The suburban middle class is increasingly multi-racial (although the pace of demographic change differs substantially across the metros). In parts of older inner-city centres and also in established African townships, the most dynamic change is an explosion of informal commercial and industrial activity. The tenacity and predictability of these developments are not surprising. They reflect the compromise central to the negotiated settlement of 1994: its terms made capital secure; it has meant that banks, building societies and other investment companies determine the pace and direction of urban change rather than the state. Changes in the built environment and urban life remain market-driven, not socially driven.[28]

These tendencies are most clearly visible in Johannesburg, South Africa's mega-city and economic hub. Jozi is the South African city on speed: edgy, hyperactive, endlessly energetic. Compared with cities anywhere in the world, Johannesburg is astonishingly protean, a metropolis with a capacity for ceaseless reinvention. Post-apartheid Johannesburg has attracted some brilliant scholarship.[29] Rather than trying to summarise it, I shall dip into its riches and pull out some illustrative plums.

Not quite a decade into the post-apartheid era, Lindsay Bremner wrote a shimmering introduction to a city in flux, its 'new geographies, new practices and new citizens'. A chapter characterised Johannesburg as 'Theme Park City': it describes Melrose Arch as a 'high-tech live/work/play' complex pretending to be a neighbourhood, but offering a 'sanitized lifestyle package' for the 'highly mobile, highly paid' post-industrial professional. Montecasino is a gambling fantasy-land in the northern suburbs, tricked out in painfully authentic fake-Tuscan detail, a palace of fun – *and* one of the world's most successful casinos. Also in the northern suburbs is Fourways Garden, laid out in 1986, and the city's first security suburb. Behind its walls and gates is 'a suburban version of the African bush', the precinct planted with indigenous trees, its nature reserve home to small buck, zebra and birds. Echoes of *Jock of the Bushveld* – but Jock drives a 4×4 and the bush is watered by sprinklers. All three of these scenic simulations 'hollow out parts of the city and … construct urban places appealing to the desire, nostalgia or paranoia of people who can pay to be there'.[30]

Bremner and Martin Murray write about another set of architectural urban forms: massive, monumental multi-block complexes housing ABSA, FNB and Standard Bank in the old Central Business District (CBD). Anyone who even visited Jo'burg in the 1990s was aware of the decay of the CBD, with the sale of the abandoned Carlton Centre symptomatic of its ills. Today at street level it remains a zone of taxi and bus queues, pavement hawkers, hucksters and hustlers; yet looming above them are the citadels of finance capital. They are in the city but not of it: they are cocooned from it by elaborate systems of underground walkways and elevated bridges. Access to the buildings is monitored, filtered, controlled. Having turned their backs on the city – its shops, services, sights, sounds and smells – these office blocks mimic city life within air-conditioned glass walls. By staying inside, a bank's employees can access an ersatz outdoors. They can go to the coffee-shop, restaurant, library, gym, hairdresser, dry-cleaner or travel agent – and much more. These buildings have translated public space into profoundly privatised milieus. They provide a kind of stage set – urban life that has been safety-curtained against urban crime and grime by the most high-tech security and surveillance systems money can buy.[31]

Fourways Garden and the bank headquarters are corporate expressions of the 'fortification aesthetic' that dominates suburban Johannesburg architecture. Its signature features are walls, electric fences, razor-wire, guard dogs, panic buttons, armed response signs – and, when the residents can afford it, the gated street or enclosed enclave. There is a savage irony to these barricades. They make prisoners of their owners. Fear of the outsider translates into fear of outdoors.

Built Johannesburg reveals new forms of closure, new technologies of exclusion, a new mapping of difference. An older racial geography, policed by curfew and *dompas*, is being supplanted by social segregation patterned on fortified enclaves, make-believe city-scapes and a no-go hinterland.

The structures described by Bremner and Murray are the progeny of capital and municipal boosterism: but there are other, countervailing forces also reshaping and reinventing Johannesburg. These are pressures from below; inchoate, dispersed, sometimes visible, frequently covert. They are exercised by those without formal political or social power; the potency of informality lies in their numbers, in the urgency of their needs, and in 'the insistence of ordinary people that they will not postpone their exercise of "the capacity to aspire"'.[32] A key site of pressures from below is the inner city of Johannesburg, which 'has changed more rapidly than perhaps any other inner city in modern history'.[33] AbdouMalik Simone argues that within a decaying physical infrastructure, there has developed a social infrastructure: a series of 'flexible, mobile, and provisional intersections' between residents, providing services and goods and opportunities. Hillbrow, Berea, Joubert Park and Yeoville house a polyglot and multinational population, some 90% of whom arrived in the past decade. They have found ways of using the urban environment, collaborating with one another. This involves a myriad interactions 'among various national and ethnic groups, between aspiring professionals and seasoned criminals, and between AIDS orphans living on the streets and wealthy Senegalese merchants'. Patterns of trade and barter, protection and pay-offs, repair and recycling of goods, drug dealing and other illicit activities: all of these, and much more, see 'people as infrastructure'. As in other African cities, these inner-city residents 'experience new forms of solidarity through their participation in makeshift, ephemeral ways of being social'.[34]

* * *

South Africa's post-apartheid cities, then, have changed in some dramatic ways, yet also demonstrate obdurate levels of continuity with the 'old' South Africa. If the country's cities are burdened by their history, they are also crucial to the future. South Africa is increasingly an urban society. Cities tend to concentrate political and social problems, and so it is in the cities that solutions must be identified, fought for and applied.

Social fault-lines
Crime, violence, anger

Policing the transition; transforming the police

Sydney Mufamadi, surely, drew the short straw. Of all the cabinet posts held by members of Mandela's new administration in 1994, his was arguably the toughest. Mufamadi, just 35 years old at the time, took office as Minister of Safety and Security, responsible for the police service. Although remembered by one of his advisers as 'charismatic, smart, self-deprecating and hard-working',[1] Mufamadi came to his portfolio with no prior knowledge of policing. He relied heavily on the group of civilians – lawyers and academics – brought into his department to advise him; but they were equally innocent of any relevant practical experience.

The size of the task faced by the minister is hinted at in the formal language of the 1996 Constitution: 'The objects of the police service are to prevent, combat and investigate crime, to maintain public order, to protect and secure the inhabitants of the RSA and their property, and to uphold and enforce the law.' In other words, his department had to decide how to police the country that the ANC now ran; it must not only fight crime and its perpetrators, but should *prevent* crime; it had to do so amidst alarmingly high levels of crime and violence (and the ANC was aware that sharp increases in crime rates had complicated transitional projects in Eastern Europe, the ex-Soviet Union and Latin American countries). The department was responsible for public order, the security of civilians, and for upholding the rule of law – as in any other modern state. But with a singular twist: the police force charged with these responsibilities must simultaneously be reformed, somehow purged of its past, and become a politically acceptable agency, in step with the political transformation that had taken place.

This was a towering challenge. The South African Police force (SAP) was central to the coercive capacity of the apartheid state. For decades it had harassed, bullied and intimidated citizens. Its core functions were keeping black people out of white areas and preventing public forms of protest. At their peak, arrests under the Pass Laws jailed millions of Africans per decade; in 1967 alone there were 700,000 convictions. For black South Africans, ordinary urban life was criminalised. Townships were policed by a series of blitzes, raids and swoops. Ordinary policing of the townships, in terms of monitoring or investigating crime, was perfunctory at best and often absent. Police officers, black and white, were distrusted and detested by

African city-dwellers; indeed, after 1976, many townships became effectively no-go zones for conventional policing. Authoritarian South Africa created a police force with a good deal of muscle, but little legitimacy. But in 1994 what was required was a police service for a democratic South Africa; one with legitimacy based on the consent of the general population. The task was nothing less than one of 'turning an army of occupation into a modern public service'.[2]

Consider the politics and the symbolism of the moment. On the one hand, ANC leaders had for decades been categorised as criminals, subversives and terrorists; membership of the organisation or 'furthering its aims' carried savage sentences. On the other hand, the officers responsible for law and order were feared and hated by many; and citizens had scant respect for a criminal justice system which for decades had prioritised repression over justice. Mufamadi himself over the years had been arrested, detained, subpoenaed and his movements restricted: an entirely predictable CV for a trade unionist and community activist. The Commissioner of Police reporting to Mufamadi was Johan van der Merwe, previously head of the Special Branch, who subsequently sought amnesty from the Truth and Reconciliation Commission (TRC) for his part in domestic bombings and cross-border raids. The new minister and his civilian staff were piloting the department through 'a sea of old blue', about 120,000 policemen and -women recruited and trained by the erstwhile enemy, their loyalty to the new regime untested and suspect.[3]

What should the new government do? One solution was offered by a senior Scotland Yard officer who spent months in the country as a Commonwealth violence monitor. 'Fire every officer from colonel to general and rebuild command and control from scratch,' he advised.[4] But of course this was not an option. Firstly, the 'sunset clause' approved during negotiations protected the jobs of the police along with those of other civil servants. Secondly, officers could not be easily replaced: the training facilities produced only a few thousand police a year. Thirdly, policing involves skills and expertise learned on the job; any exodus of officers also meant losing institutional memory and capacity (as happened, when many white officers took retrenchment packages or resigned). And, finally, while the ANC possessed a guerrilla army and negotiated over its integration with the Defence Force, it had no equivalent police force. 'It was quite different from the army,' recalled Albie Sachs; 'the issue was transforming the SAP and integrating all the different police units, rather than establishing a new police force.'[5] The integration to which he referred involving melding no fewer than 11 police forces, including those from the homeland structures, the municipal police and the notorious *kitskonstabels*: these elements composed almost 50% of the personnel of the amalgamated force.

So, as the ANC prepared to govern, its thinking about the police was shaped by two very different imperatives. The first was the reform of the police force, releasing it from an authoritarian past into a future in which its practices and operations marched in step with human rights and democracy. The ANC's thinking in this regard was strongly influenced by an international shift in attitudes at the end of the Cold War. 'Police forces were suddenly discovered as protectors of rights. They were identified as important cornerstones for enabling the rule of law', protecting the citizenry, and guaranteeing stability.[6] The second was an anxiety about rising levels of crime, sharpened by incessant reminders that crime had spiralled to new heights in other infant democracies. This anxiety translated into a desire to have policing that was more effective, better equipped to defend people and property. These two imperatives were not easily addressed together: prioritising either one threatened to weaken the other. The ANC, in hindsight, underestimated how difficult it would be to succeed in addressing either, let alone both.

The Government of National Unity (GNU) which took office in 1994 inherited a police force that would continue to be run by the same senior officers, shaped by the same institutional culture. To offset this legacy, the GNU effected changes in governance, in culture and in policy. Firstly, it attempted to exercise a greater degree of civilian control over the police than the NP government had done. The key instruments were an Independent Complaints Directorate; Community Police Forums (a constitutional requirement); and a civilian Secretariat within the Department of Safety and Security. Secondly, with support from the upper echelons of the SAP, it initiated a series of symbolic changes intended to dramatise the break with the past. The SAP force became the South African Police Service (SAPS); new uniforms, vehicle colours and ranks were consciously less 'military'; each new name and symbol was ceremonially and publicly launched. The new culture was bolstered by the establishment of a Human Rights and Policing Programme, with an ambitious training brief.

Thirdly, in the sphere of policy, a 'host of foreign governments, criminologists and think tanks descended on South African shores' while senior police managers 'eager to recalibrate their ideas to the new order … did serial study tours to Europe and North America'. The key outcome of these exchanges was an enthusiastic embrace by the new government of two key policy directions: 'community policing' and 'crime prevention'.[7] The central idea of community-oriented policing is that police should be constantly visible and in contact with community members. The main shape that this policy took was the establishment of a Community Police Forum in every district served by a police station, although other formal and informal links were established too. The core statement of crime prevention was the 1996 National

Crime Prevention Strategy. The NCPS was an open-minded and ambitious attempt to identify the causes of crime – social, structural, historical – and to specify forms of state intervention to combat these causes. It was holistic, specifying that 'Crime needs to be tackled in a comprehensive way, which means going beyond an exclusive focus on policing and the justice system'. It was vauntingly optimistic: 'nothing less than a paean to the transformative powers of government'. It specified roles across half a dozen departments, with dozens of agencies at every tier of government – but the strategy was essentially stillborn. Departments of Health, Transport, Welfare and so forth had their hands full with their own responsibilities; they had little inclination to tackle crime prevention too.[8]

The NCPS remained prominent on the department's website; but in practice was increasingly sidelined, especially by its replacement in 2000 with the National Crime Combating Strategy – which differs from the NCPS 'by one word and an ocean of ideology'. The two words reveal a good deal, remarks Ted Leggett: '"prevention" calls to mind a public health approach; "combating" has distinct military undertones.'[9] The NCCS document was one important marker by the Mbeki presidency of a new stance on policing; another was his first State of the Nation address, in which he announced the formation of the Scorpions to fight crime. They were accompanied by the appointment of Steve Tshwete as Minister and

Jackie Selebi as National Police Commissioner – Mbeki men, charged with being tough on crime. The NCCS was driven by the desire to reduce crime, to change the crime statistics that had become so highly politicised that a moratorium was placed on their issue for 18 months.

Over the next five years there was a realignment of the SAPS, a reversion to paramilitary policing in the name of crime prevention ('We are going to deal with criminals as a bulldog does with a bull,' growled Tshwete). The strategy targeted 140 police stations – one in ten – which account for more than 50% of serious crime, and applied 'saturation policing' to them, deploying police and military. Police presence was concentrated around crime 'hotspots' and interventions took the form of traditional, authoritarian policing. Thus, 'The police and the military show up in force. They make themselves visible. They wake everyone up at three a.m. and search their sugar bowls, without specific probable cause. They arrest people who arouse their suspicions ... They seize lots of undocumented people and guns ... They throw up roadblocks and cordon-and-search operations ... This return to militaristic policing should surprise no one. To a man with a hammer, everything looks like a nail.'[10]

There is a consensus that in the first Mbeki presidency, crime prevention was 'sidelined in favour of short-term and tougher approaches', including longer minimum sentences and aggressive policing.[11] Jonny Steinberg argues that, ironically, the ANC's embrace of crime prevention had unintended consequences; that the crime prevention approach emphasised urban security; and that 'a malevolent and bloated conception of security that had seeped into urban culture during apartheid' now drove post-apartheid policing. An imported tool-kit was selectively applied in favour of paramilitary policing aimed at rounding up young black men. Policing under an ANC government came to 'mimic in eerie and disturbing fashion the paramilitary policing practices that evolved at the high tide of white minority rule'.[12]

These tendencies were accelerated in 2008–9 when Mbeki was succeeded by Zuma as President. Under Zuma, the 'war against crime' was beefed up rhetorically and substantively. Charles Nqakula became Minister of Safety and Security when Tshwete died in 2002; four years later he won media attention by promising that 'Anyone who points a firearm at police will be killed by police officers'. His deputy, Susan Shabangu, caused a greater stir in April 2008 when she addressed an anti-crime meeting in unambiguous terms: 'You must kill the bastards [criminals] if they threaten you or the community. You must not worry about the regulations. I want no warning shots. You have one shot and it must be a kill shot ... I want to assure the police station commissioners and policemen and women ... that they have permission to kill these criminals.'

By the time Shabangu was promoted by Zuma as Minister of Mineral and Energy Affairs, policing was headed by Nathi Mthethwa as Minister and Bheki Cele as National Police Commissioner. Both men were from KwaZulu-Natal; both had been staunch Zuma supporters during the rivalry with Mbeki. A series of easy-to-read symbolic changes were announced. Mthethwa was originally appointed as Minister of Safety and Security; but now he became Minister of Police. The Commissioner would henceforth be called General and the older military ranks were reinstated.

Telling as these semantic revisions were, they were less important than steps taken to give the police more authority, more weapons and more licence in the 'war against crime'. In 2009 Cele created a new set of specialised units, the Tactical Response Teams (TRTs). Initially directed against cash-in-transit gangs, the TRTs were based on the thesis that a really hardened criminal core is relatively small; a specialist, highly armed force to combat specialist, highly armed crime. In the months that followed their formation, the TRT activities against criminals effectively blurred the line between policing and warfare, and some of their operations looked startlingly like extra-judicial executions. In its first four months, the TRTs killed 50 alleged criminals. In 2009, police killed 556 people – the highest total since 1994. But the TRTs' mandate combined responsibility for the 'combating of crime' with the 'maintenance of public order'. Especially during 2011, there was a series of protests that the units were using excessive force to disperse municipal or 'service delivery' protests. Especially from Mpumalanga there were claims that the TRT – its members called the Amaberete for their black-and-red berets – left chaos in its wake.[13]

In January 2011 the Operational Response Services component of the SAPS was established as a full police division, the Operational Service Division. Its units include the TRTs, a National Intervention Unit and the Special Task Force. It was members of the new division who killed the unarmed Andries Tatane in a dusty township street outside Ficksburg in April 2011 – and made the mistake of doing so in view of television cameramen, provoking widespread outrage. Members of these units were amongst the 6000 police deployed at Marikana in August 2012. By then – David Bruce has shown – Minister Mthethwa had several times spoken of the need to use 'maximum force against violent criminals and minimum force in dealing with fellow citizens'. But this distinction was lost when – on 17 August 2012, the day after the Marikana massacre – the new National Police Commissioner, Riah Phiyega, stated that the police 'were forced to use maximum force to defend themselves'. Earlier in the same year, the National Assembly amended section 49 of the Criminal Procedure Act, expanding police powers to use 'lethal force' to apprehend those suspected of serious violent crime. 'There is little pleasure to be had', comments Bruce bleakly, 'in the irony that the amendment passed its final hurdle in the parliamentary process ... on 16 August 2012, the same day as the Marikana massacre.'[14]

Focusing solely on the police force might convey the impression that they alone are involved in policing, but this is far from the case. Because many members of the public remain unconvinced that they are afforded appropriate protection by the police, there has been a massive growth of alternative forms of security. The private security sector has grown exponentially since the 1970s and is believed to be the largest in the world in terms of its contribution to GDP – about 2%. There are just under 9000 registered security businesses and 411,000 active registered security officers (by comparison, there are 1125 police stations and 163,000 policemen and -women). Such companies patrol and guard public space – streets, shopping malls, business districts – and also provide high levels of private security – installing high-tech alarms and responding when these are triggered, as well as patrolling and gate-keeping privatised space like gated communities.[15] In addition to private security firms, there is a broad spectrum of civilian forms of self-organisation for security. These range from suburban 'neighbourhood watch' exercises to formal groupings of local traders or residents, to more loosely structured street committees, and, at the spectrum's end, various forms of localised and unapproved vigilante action, which are frequently expressed as punitive violence meted out to suspected criminals. These forms of civic security sometimes work in partnership with the police; sometimes with formal or informal approval by the local police; and sometimes entirely independently.

One way of thinking about South Africa's policing since 1994 is to imagine two parallel worlds. In one, the police force is remade, modelled on best practice internationally; its members behave 'with compassion, professionalism and integrity',[16] winning respect, authority and legitimacy in the process. In that world, crime prevention is a holistic, whole-of-society project: enhanced investigative capacity of the police and a swift, reliable justice system are complemented by comprehensive, targeted interventions to alter the social environment that breeds crime. In that world, community policing is central: 'participation by communities and community policing form the bedrock of effective law enforcement'. Such policing would be driven by a service ethic, partnerships, problem-solving, empowerment and accountability. All police members would 'develop new skills through training which incorporates problem solving, networking, mediation, facilitation, conflict resolution and community involvement'.[17]

In the second, parallel, world, police officers were never easy clay for the policy potters. Their institutional culture was resistant; their skills remained limited or deficient; their training fell wildly short of the enhanced role they were supposed to discharge. Faced with the disparity between what was expected of them and what they felt they could do, ordinary police members fell back on what they knew best – they resorted to violence, allowing them 'the illusion of efficiency and potency';[18] they avoided administrative chores whenever they could; and developed informal and ad hoc relations with members of the public – which could all too easily involve a trade of favours and cash. It is easy to be dispirited by the story of policing in South Africa since 1994, but it is important to remember that policemen and -women are individuals with the whole range of human virtues and vices – and we are fortunate to possess outstanding ethnographies of police working in this second world.[19] These remind us that 'cops are loved and hated, praised and blamed', enjoying 'fragile, untrusting and fluid' relations with their local communities.[20]

In this second world, neither crime prevention nor community policing lived up to the idealistic intentions of the first. Crime prevention was shorn of its holistic promise, and narrowed to a project of law enforcement, a 'return to basics', in which police would be given more recruits and larger budgets in the fight against crime. This was a contest the police could not win: it pitted the agency at the symptoms and not the causes of crime. Community policing fared little better: five years after its official launch as the core focus of policing, it was abandoned 'or at best simply ignored or disregarded ... throughout the SAPS'.[21] Some gains have been made, even in the second world. An assessment of the SAPS in 2007 praised its record in protecting and supporting democracy, and found, overall, 'substantial progress and numerous achievements in the process of police reform'. However, the report found the greatest shortcomings in the area of appropriate police conduct. There was evidence of pervasive corruption and rising levels of reported police brutality.[22] Since 2007, corruption has not been checked and the abuse of 'lethal power' has become a major issue. In many communities, police members are still disliked, distrusted and feared. The gap between the worlds of aspiration and reality has become a gulf.

Crime and criminality in the 'new South Africa'

Crime, and the fear of crime, preoccupies many South African households. It is a staple of letters to the press, radio phone-ins and dinner party exchanges. For the past twenty years, crime has particularly concerned middle-class suburbanites: this reflects the changing social geography of crime. In the post-apartheid city, violent crime has spilled out of the townships, where it was historically contained, and invaded the suburbs. At the same time, although they are less audible in the national conversation on crime, working-class and poor households – without access to private security or alarm systems – actually experience crime more frequently and more severely. Crime and policing have become highly charged and politicised over the past two decades. Much of the macho bluster that propelled the recourse to militarised policing was a political response to popular and media concerns; reducing crime has been identified by the Zuma government as one of its top five priorities; and a majority of the population approve of tougher policing.

The national preoccupation with crime is especially intense, once a year, when the crime statistics are released. These figures are received with a morbid fascination, strongly laced with suspicion and scepticism as to their accuracy. In reality, every government, when it presents crime statistics to its citizens and their media, casts them in as favourable a light as possible. They emphasise some aspects and try to blur others. Governments routinely massage crime data, but they do not fabricate data. This is the case in South Africa, too: the annual figures are manipulated but not manufactured. They are by international standards relatively robust, and are more systematically collected and collated than they were before 1994.

The most recent figures available are those for the financial year 2011/12, and can be located within a broader story: the changing pattern of crime over the past twenty years. Take the crucial and sensitive measure: the murder rate. There were 15,609 reported murders in the year, 3.1% down from the previous year or an average of 43 murders a day for a year. This is a shocking rate. There were more murders in South Africa that year – just a straight body-count – than in the USA, with a population six times as large and a well-earned reputation as a violent society. Comparative murder rates are usually expressed as instances per 100,000 of the population. South Africa's murder rate is about 41 per 100,000: eight times higher than that of the USA, twenty times higher than Western Europe, eighty times higher than Japan.

However, despite these grim comparisons, the murder rate in South Africa is falling quite sharply. The drop of 3% in 2011/12 occurred within an overall drop of just over 40% since 1995/6. In that year, there were nearly 27,000 murders, or 69 a day. In fact, all so-called contact crimes (murder, attempted murder, grievous bodily harm, common assault, aggravated robbery and sexual offences) are down by 35% from 2004/5 levels. Within contact crimes, sexual offences remain dismayingly and stubbornly high; there were 64,000 reported sexual assaults in 2011/12; the number of rapes fell by only 1.7%. To return to the murder statistics: who is killing whom, and why has the rate dropped so significantly? Young, black males are most liable to violent death: 38% of all homicide victims are aged between 20 and 29; and two-thirds of all homicide victims are aged between 20 and 39. Young black (African and coloured) men are significantly more at risk. As Jonny Steinberg puts it, 'While one in nine South Africans is white, 32 out of 33 murder victims aren't.'[23] A distinctive feature of South African murder is that 88% of victims and 94% of perpetrators are male – both higher than the global average. About two-thirds of all murders were the result of arguments, confrontations and domestic violence; the other third spread between murder in the course of sexual assault, murder in the course of robbery and murders in conflicts over territory, markets and power – gang wars, taxi wars.[24]

There is no definitive answer as to why the murder level has fallen so significantly, but Antony Altbeker has suggested two factors that help explain it. The increased spending by government on social services – the income provided through grants and pensions – may have helped stabilise some households, especially the poorest, taking the edge off extreme need and thus reducing the likelihood of killings based in domestic rows. He also argues that the decline in political violence since 1994 may be a factor: 'it is possible that cycles of violence are being dampened as distance from the direct experience of violence grows.' Optimistically, he wonders if 'the habits of moderation, self-regulation, compromise and self-control – the habits that come from living in a less volatile society – have begun to take hold'.

This points us towards a further, inescapable aspect of criminality in South Africa. Altbeker quotes an American criminologist who found that 'the distinctive feature of crime in South Africa is not its volume but its violence'. Altbeker concurs: 'Our murder rate is exceptionally high by world standards. So, too, is the robbery rate, especially the armed variety. Property crime that involves no violence, by contrast, is no worse than in other countries.

As a nation … our problem is an unhealthy addiction to violence, not to law-breaking in general.'[25]

Why this is so is a hugely complex question. Any attempt to answer it briefly must oversimplify – and what follows is just such an oversimplification. But there is a convergence in thinking in existing studies that any answer to the question must have three main components: the legacy of the past; the pressures of inequality and exclusion; and a culture of criminality.

Over twenty years ago, Shula Marks and Neil Anderssen insisted that political violence in the late 1980s must be located within a wider social and historical context. 'South Africa is a very violent society … the culture of violence exists at every level.' Overt political violence is just one more of many forms of endemic violence. Industrialisation and urbanisation – they note – have caused poverty, social dislocation and stress in many societies. In South Africa, industrialisation was built upon migrant labour; urbanisation on the basis of segregation and exclusion. As segregation hardened into apartheid, a dense thicket of laws controlled and regimented black life. Insecurity, harassment and petty violence were pervasive. Apartheid was a major source of violence because of the stress and tension it generated; because it destroyed family life and community networks; and because it impacted adversely on the physical and psycho-social health of the black population. Their conclusion is sobering: 'The social distortions that have resulted – what we have called the culture of violence – are likely to outlive the dismantling of the institutions that called them into being.'[26]

Their findings have been amplified, but never refuted. Gary Kynoch compared urban violence in Johannesburg (including criminal violence, gang conflict and vigilantism) in the 1950s and 1960s with violence in other colonial African cities. He shows that Johannesburg's townships were experiencing destabilising crime problems from the 1950s; and that violent crime rose steadily and steeply from the mid-1950s to the mid-1990s. At the heart of his findings is that 'Simply put, South Africa's mining industry served as an incubator for violence'. A grid of institutions emerged around the mining industry and consequent industrialisation: compounds for male migrant workers, criminal gangs and vigilantes in segregated townships, and a teeming prison population that mixed pass law offenders with hardened criminals.[27]

Secondly, there is an historical and a current link between inequality and social exclusion, on the one hand, and violence, on the other. This relationship is not peculiar to South Africa, as a body of comparative evidence indicates that the link is real. Altbeker (although his best-known book on crime reaches a different conclusion) actually proposed in 2008 that 'inequality is at the root of South Africa's crime problems'. This is not only because of the extent of inequality in the country, 'but because of the character of inequality in South Africa – which is driven by the systematic exclusion of millions of people from participation in the labour market', shaping perceptions of the gap between the promise of equality and the lived reality of inequality. This drives crime by creating a set of incentives that leads some poor people to choose the benefits of crime over the hard slog of trying to 'stay straight'.[28]

Inequality and social exclusion impact directly on the third broad reason for the violence of crime in South Africa: the development and persistence within youth gangs of a culture or sub-culture of criminality. Clive Glaser is the historian of the urban *tsotsi* and he emphasises that urban African families faced acute difficulties almost from their inception. Gender imbalance, the prevalence of single-parent families, the loss of kinship links operating in rural areas, and weak parental supervision meant that the family played a diminished socialising role. Alternative sources of socialisation were few: where else might urban African teenagers learn restraint, find role models, identify with the broader society, gain any sense of a meaningful future? Three possibilities were churches, schools and gangs. In Soweto, schools briefly offered a credible alternative to gangs, providing role models and activities. But in the 1970s, the black education system fell apart, and schools were largely discredited for the Soweto generation. For many young males, it was juvenile gangs that provided a sense of solidarity and identity. Gang membership conferred 'social respect, even if generated largely through fear', and self-respect. In the longer run, 'the gang remains an extraordinarily attractive structure for young urban men who cannot relate to, and see no future in, more socially integrative institutions'.[29]

The sub-culture of *tsotsi* and other youth gangs, historically, hardened into more explicitly criminal gangsterism. For David Bruce, although violence in South Africa is multi-faceted, 'The core of the problem is a culture of violence and criminality, which is most concentrated in metropolitan areas and which involves young men who are engaged in active criminal lifestyles … Within the peer networks in which they are situated, credibility is partly earned by demonstrating the readiness to resort to extreme violence with a weapon.'[30] Criminal gangs are characterised by aggressive male identity; by a materialist desire for consumer goods; and by a code that valorises, or endorses, violence as a means of acquiring status. It is a culture of macho unruliness, fuelled by an almost insatiable appetite for money, luxuries and women.

Such a culture is captured in an unforgettable account of a Soweto gangster's funeral by Antony Altbeker. The man being buried had been shot at a failed cash-in-transit heist. The funeral procession 'was part carnival, part rodeo and part shebeen'. Expensive cars, with young women hanging from open windows, careered along the road to the cemetery, their drivers weaving in and out of traffic.

It was a 'gluttonous excess of psychotic merriment'.[31] The young people strutting their stuff at the graveside embodied the distinctive sub-culture. Disdainful of law and responsibility, they exhibited an aggressive disregard of the lives and property of others. They were mourning a death, but celebrating a lifestyle.

'Angry people are not always wise' (Jane Austen)

Crime and violence are inextricably linked in South Africa – and violence is first cousin to anger. Jonathan Jansen asked a few years ago: 'Why are South Africans so angry? We not only protest, we also burn down and break down; we turn over garbage cans and beat each other senseless with chains at political rallies; we threaten, and yes, we kill. We slander and we demean … Where does this deep-seated anger come from? Why are we so prone to what appears to be spontaneous combustion?' He answered his own question: 'the anger comes from somewhere deep within ourselves and our history … nothing compares with the anger and brutality of the rainbow nation.'[32] That history (if reminder were needed) included colonial conquest, slavery, frontier wars and dispossession. It is a history of social exclusion and racial separation; of economic exploitation through cheap and coerced labour; and a politics that arrogated power to the few to dominate the many. It makes for an historical legacy that cannot be wished away. It has to be confronted, if it is to be overcome.

This history has created in contemporary South Africa a profoundly racialised society, in two obvious and important ways. Firstly, privilege, possessions and power are distributed along largely racial lines. White South Africans are *structurally* and historically the beneficiaries of apartheid and minority rule. Secondly, South African identities, behaviours and beliefs are strongly inflected by race and racial perceptions. When South Africans are invited to reflect upon themselves and their society, 'Everything is filtered through a racial lens ... the national public discourse remains obsessed with race.' This judgement was made in the context of a fascinating, and important, set of discussions in the shape of eighteen focus groups staged across South Africa in mid-2011.[33]

While racialised thinking has been prevalent ever since 1994, its content and character have shifted. In the early years of Mandela's presidency, there was a brief, heady euphoria around the notion of a rainbow nation – but it was short-lived. Its demise was hastened by the failure of white South Africans to respond adequately or appropriately to the TRC – a failure which reportedly brought Tutu to tears and stirred Mandela to anger. White South Africans, for the most part, were content to have blame attached to several thousand named 'perpetrators' of human rights abuse and to assume their own blamelessness. Yet, as the TRC itself pointed out, 'The result is that ordinary South Africans do not see themselves as represented by those the Commission defines as perpetrators, failing to recognise the "little perpetrator" in all of us.' (There were strong echoes of this in 2011, when Desmond Tutu remarked that it would be appropriate to tax white South Africans for the benefits that they had received from apartheid – and was met with a storm of indignation and denial.)

And, as the rainbow faded, Thabo Mbeki spearheaded a very different call to nationhood: one that celebrated an African renaissance and asserted that national identity should be constructed around the culture and values of the majority. His own measured stance was soon translated by intellectuals and journalists in his camp into a strident, assertive and exclusive Africanism. Xolela Mangcu called it 'racial nativism'. 'This is the idea that the true custodians of African culture are the natives. The natives are often defined as black Africans because they are indigenous to the country, and within that group the true natives are those who participated in the resistance struggle. And even among those who participated in the liberation, the truest natives are those who are on the side of government. By dint of their authenticity these natives have the right to silence white interlopers or black sell-outs.'

Mangcu also posits a link between racial nativism and white denial: 'There is a certain smugness and lack of contrition in the white community that is oftentimes quite breathtaking ... This culture of denial and racial solidarity among whites provides the backdrop for understanding why black nativist leaders are able to entrench themselves further in power.' T.O. Molefe made the same connection: between what he styled 'Black anger and white obliviousness'.[34]

Today, South Africa has a colour-blind constitution, is publicly committed to non-racialism, and swathes of discriminatory legislation have been repealed. Yet notions of race remain tenacious, pernicious and pervasive. South Africans find it difficult to think about themselves and their fellow citizens other than in race terms. 'It seems that every South African ... can reel off a litany of racial slights, real or imagined; see positive and negative discrimination all about them.' In the focus group project mentioned above, several themes emerged. The men and women involved in the discussions spoke frequently of their deep-seated angers, fears and tensions about race: but they also recognised that they are trapped in such thinking and seek to escape it. 'Citizens may not know what non-racialism means, nor how to provide a robust definition of the term, but they know intuitively that it is the only route to a secure future for all South Africans.' Accordingly, they take tentative, experimental steps across racial boundaries; adults speak of 'how their children mix freely and "don't see race"'; many members of the focus groups 'appear to be trying to find ways to inch towards each other'; and they are doing so with precious little leadership by politicians. David Everatt's conclusion is cogent: 'Racism and race obsession is fuelled by inequality – social as well as economic – and if the non-racial project is not about redistribution and attacking inequality, it will fail ... Non-racialism needs to be active, proactive, and attack the current status quo ... If South Africa really does belong to all who live in it, black and white, then all those who live in it, black and white, need to be equal.'[35]

In 1954 the trade unionist Naboth Mokgatle – after receiving a banning order – entered exile and went to live in London. He found it difficult to adjust. 'When people live in a concentration camp, where they are denied human rights and live in a terror of mass ill-treatment, their nervous system is destroyed, and their power to think like other human beings is destroyed as well ... [In London] I was like a person who had been sick for a very long time ... My sickness was a very old one and my cure was long.'[36] Apartheid is over. White minority rule came to an end in 1994. But the psychic damage – Mokgatle's very old disease – has not been cured. When David Smith, currently the *Guardian* correspondent in South Africa, had been in South Africa for just five months, he wrote an article headed 'Apartheid may have been excised, but the scars still itch in unequal South Africa'. The article ends with these words: 'I remember a cynic whispering in my ear: "The whites are pretending it didn't happen; the blacks are pretending to forgive."' I suspect that very few South Africans can read those words without a spasm of recognition. A couple of weeks after Smith's article, Njabulo Ndebele wrote a wonderful piece in response. He acknowledges the forms of pretence that Smith identified, and argues that they created spaces of anguish in which South Africans are locked by their past. And he muses on the negotiated settlement and the 1994 elections: 'It seems as if instead of setting out to create a new reality, we worked merely to inherit an old one … we reaffirmed the structures of inequality by seeking to work within their inherent logic.'

In an arresting passage, Ndebele asks how South Africans can discover a commonality, how they can build 'social solidarity across the great barriers of race, ethnicity, gender and class', and find 'an appropriate political instrument that will set a foundation of trust for South Africans to recover their shared idealism'. And his answer is: 'First, the existence of such a collective space of anguish may have to be recognised and acknowledged as the one feature in our public and private lives that has the potential to bind us.' Neville Alexander pursued a similar logic. The key question was 'how to move towards understanding without ever forgetting, but to remember without constantly rekindling the divisive passions of the past'. Such an approach would allow South Africans to 'look downwards into the darkness of the well of the atrocities of the past … at the same time as we haul up the waters of hope for a future of dignity and equality'.[37]

Ndebele and Alexander both advocate engagement with the legacy of the past as a necessary route to the possibility of a different future.

Change and continuity
Some conclusions

> **transform** *vt* to change the shape of; to change
> *esp* radically or thoroughly to another form,
> appearance, substance or character
> **transformation** *n* the act of transforming; a
> change of form, constitution or substance
> *– Chambers Dictionary*

Once upon a time – twenty years ago, to be precise – South
Africa was on the brink of transformation. The ANC said
so, over and over again. President Mandela said so: 'Our
country is going through a profound transformation
at all levels of government and society … This
transformation will permeate every level of government,
every department, and every public institution.' The
Reconstruction and Development Programme, said the
RDP White Paper, provided 'a vision for the fundamental
transformation of South Africa'. The ANC contested the
1994 election on the ultimate promise of transformation:

'a better life for all'. The pledge of change hung like ripe fruit: government, economy and society would be transformed. A tireless agenda would transform housing, schooling, health and welfare; a transformative wand would be waved over police and army and civil service; a nation would change its beliefs and its behaviour, decked in rainbow hues.

The call for transformation promised too much – and too little. It promised too much, because many of those uttering the call knew perfectly well that the negotiated settlement imposed formidable limits on what the ANC could actually change, let alone change fundamentally or radically. They knew that the transition and the 1994 election did not herald fundamental shifts in the distribution of social or economic power; that the state had not been dismantled, but taken over more or less intact, under new management; and that as far as the economy went (as a key insider put it) 'this was not a promising moment for the new government to attempt to implement new policies or programmes'.[1] Invoking transformation also promised too little, because it did not specify exactly what would be changed, how, or when. Wielding transformation as a slogan drained it of meaning as a programme.

Once the dust of the 1994 election had settled, a telling semantic shift took place. The term 'transformation' was central in 'the languages of post-apartheid politics'. Indeed, mused Thiven Reddy, why '"transformation" has taken centre-stage to represent a notion of social change, and not competing signifiers such as "structural change", "radical change", "liberation" or "revolution" – words that traditionally resonate with the language of the struggle against apartheid – is an interesting question'.[2] While 'transformation' became the indispensable concept of political discourse, it acquired new meanings. It became unthreatening and conventional, shorn of associations with struggle and resistance. Today 'even opposition parties schooled in Afrikaner nationalist and conservative liberal frameworks rely on its power to make their utterances "reasonable", understandable and legitimate'. 'Transformation' no longer suggests the possibility of 'fundamental' change, but 'suggests and defines the limits of the "acceptable" in post-apartheid political language'.[3]

The most sustained engagement with the shifting meanings of 'transformation' has been the trenchant blog 'Constitutionally Speaking' by Pierre de Vos. Since 2009, he has criticised the tendency to reduce transformation to a synonym for affirmative action, 'a demand for the transfer of political, legal and economic power from one racial elite to another'. In 2010 he suggested that the term was often used 'as a band-aid to hide and legitimise the continued injustice and inequality that is perpetrated by the old business elite and the new political and business elite'. A year later, he warmed to his theme. The term was bandied about 'as if transformation is about replacing reactionary middle aged white patriarchs with reactionary middle aged black patriarchs'.[4]

What has occurred is not only a discursive shift, but an ideological lurch away from any hint of structural change. Google the words 'South Africa transformation': in the first handful of entries are such radicals as the multinational financial services giant Deloitte ('committed to equal opportunity', wishing 'to be a fully transformed, honest and vibrant representative of the South African community') and Anglo American (whose 'transformation journey is underpinned by Anglo American's values and business principles'). Transformation has been divested of radicalism and reduced to head counts, 'a "numbers game", in which "representivity" is the key term'.[5]

* * *

The limits to transformation – the extent to which expectations of more fundamental change have not been met – are complex and important. In part, the *expectations* of transformation in 1994 were unrealistic. In part, change was constrained by policy priorities and choices made by the ANC government. But to a significant degree, change was compromised by forces over which government had less control. These included the global context in which decisions were made and priorities set; the workings of a capitalist economy strongly shaped by its past and increasingly subject to decisions made elsewhere; issues of state capacity; and the outcomes of class formation and changing social relations in the not-so-new South Africa. It is also worth noting that some of the changes that *have* taken place are hardest to quantify but nonetheless real. These are in the realm of consciousness; they are to do with 'dignity and agency': even within stunted social and economic transformation, millions of people have a new sense of self-worth and capacity.[6] These are the subjective corollary to formal or constitutional inclusion.

Global context – and a built-in bias

The global context has shaped the ANC's capacity as government in several ways. Firstly, as argued in Chapter 1, the concessions made by the ANC during negotiations – in favour of capitalist continuity, away from redistribution – reflected an international balance of forces tilted quite strongly against left-wing elements in the developing world. Secondly, having committed in advance to balanced budgets, fiscal prudence and liberalising the economy, the ANC once in office could operate only within what Gramsci called 'the limits of the possible'. Having relaxed capital controls, the ANC could not prevent capital flight as the largest corporations globalised their operations, listed on European stock exchanges, and transferred vast amounts of wealth out of the country. Capital flowed out of the economy far faster than foreign investment trickled in. Having liberalised tariffs, the ANC had to watch the domestic textile industry hammered by cheap imports, and hundreds of thousands of jobs shed in manufacturing industries.

Thirdly, many aspects of the South African economy simply mirrored those taking place in capitalist economies across the world. Internationally, over the past several decades, the 'logic of the market' has seen increased inequality, an accelerated casualisation of labour and rising unemployment. In the boom years, domestic economies depend upon property and commodity bubbles, private indebtedness, and the consumption of luxury items. South Africa, since 1994, has replicated every one of these features. And South Africans who have benefited by these developments have tended (like their international counterparts) increasingly to regard them as normal, as 'the way things are'. And if this is the way things are, what benefit is there in resisting them or seeking an alternative? To lapse so easily into the circularity of 'market forces common sense' is not only lazy, but it also closes off other ways of thinking about South Africa's challenges and solutions.

Fourthly, this common sense – the ideological and intellectual context of the age – means that there is a stock of ready-made solutions, tried-and-tested options, for almost every area of policy. South African policy-makers, like their counterparts elsewhere, drew upon an imported conceptual tool-kit. Community policing and crime prevention; Outcomes Based Education; managerialist techniques and precepts in universities; new public management; public–private partnerships; the doctrines of 'cost recovery' and 'user pays' in the delivery of public services; calls for greater 'flexibility' in the labour market – these are only a few examples of 'solutions' engineered in the advanced capitalist economies.

The state of the state

The ANC has wrestled for years with how to define itself vis-à-vis the capitalist economic order in which it holds office. As noted in Chapter 2, since about 2004 it has sought to differentiate its approach from that of a neo-liberal capitalist state by announcing that it would become a developmental state – more interventionist, more autonomous from capital.[7] Distancing himself from the earlier 'fundamentalist' phase of GEAR, Mbeki in his second term nudged policy towards what Adam Habib neatly captures as 'neo-liberalism with a human face'. Zuma's administration has extended policy adjustments begun under Mbeki: attempts to revive industry, the expansion of the social welfare system, a public works programme funded in part by allowing budget deficits to rise. Habib suggests that it is 'groping towards social democracy'.[8]

In 2009 the ANC election manifesto promised that 'The developmental state will play a central and strategic role in the economy. We will ensure a more effective government.' But the record of its second decade in office suggests that the ANC fails as a developmental state on both these counts – reshaping the economy and running an effective government. Zuma's government remains impaled on the same contradiction that constrained Mbeki's: the commitment to macroeconomic stability remains the trump card. Treasury overrides spending departments; and (as in the National Development Plan) the ANC's current version of a 'better life for all' rests ultimately on trickle-down economics, on growth before redistribution. The ANC in government has not struck a new deal with big business, 'coaxing or coercing private capital to invest' in domestic growth, but has instead aided capital flight and left the giant conglomerates free of responsibility for domestic accumulation.[9]

Secondly, successful developmental states (including the original 'East Asian Tigers' and contemporary 'democratic developmental states') had the capacity to design, implement and administer their policies: that is, they relied on well-functioning state departments staffed by meritocratic civil servants. 'A development state requires an intellectual, cultural and philosophical shift that South Africa has not yet made,' judged Roger Southall. 'In such a state, the state bureaucracy is composed of the nation's brightest and best, following administrative careers which are not subject to the whims of political fortune.'[10] The South African departments of state and their civil servants, in many instances, fail this test. There are any number of accounts that suggest this failure is almost entirely to do with rushed and top-heavy affirmative action: that 'representivity' has defeated efficiency. Such explanation is intellectually lazy, and often racist in tone and assumptions.

Any considered account of the poor performance of the public service, at all levels of government, would factor in other causes. First, the post-apartheid bureaucracy had a far wider remit than its apartheid predecessor, which 'existed primarily to provide services to its White constituency'. The post-apartheid state in effect 'increased its target group from four to 44 million. This in turn requires a far more capacitated public service. The public sector is struggling to adapt to this gargantuan challenge.'[11] This challenge was accentuated, especially between 1996 and 2003, when the ANC's concern to control public spending meant failing to fill vacant posts in many departments. Further, Ivor Chipkin has argued convincingly that the rise of New Public Management in departments of state has compounded the skills deficit by a new emphasis on managerialism rather than administration, raising the bar of what was required from senior civil servants at precisely the same time as the drive to repopulate their ranks with more black members.[12] Finally, state capacity has been seriously eroded by the ANC's inability or unwillingness to rein in corruption and graft by its own members 'deployed' to public service.

How successfully, then, has the ANC 'groped towards social democracy'? In its own account, the ANC 'leans towards the poor', 'recognises the leading role of the working class in … social transformation', is 'a disciplined force of the left' and 'approximates, in many respects, the best elements of a developmental state and social democracy'. This combines the movement's habitual and increasingly hollow left-rhetoric with a rather wistful optimism: 'approximates, in many respects'. In which respects, one has to wonder, does the ANC project not 'approximate' a developmental state or social democracy? No amount of huffing and puffing about the disparity between a 'first' and 'second' economy should disguise the fact that it is precisely the workings of the capitalist economy, as currently structured, which help create poverty and joblessness for half the population. Nor can any degree of leaning towards the poor (let alone recognising working-class leadership!) disguise the fact that there is by now a sizeable component of the ANC political and business elite that would resist any efforts to alter the status quo meaningfully. Many senior ANC officials have significant business interests; and South African business leaders have a shared set of views about taxes, regulation and the labour market, 'whatever their pigmentation'.[13]

In a class of their own?

In 2004 Linda Chisholm edited an important collection of studies on education and social change in the first post-apartheid decade. 'The major conclusion emerging from the book', she noted in her Introduction, 'is both simple and dramatic. Educational development and the emerging system have favoured an expanding, racially-mixed middle class.' Favouring the middle class was not the conscious intent of policy; but 'whatever the gap between intent and outcomes, there is no doubt that the resulting social change is considerable in achievement and direction'.[14] Middle-class parents and children benefited substantially in various ways. The introduction of school fees proved a major differentiator. While most township and rural schools were exempt from fees, those able to charge fees could appoint extra teachers, run additional activities, and generally enhance the learning experience for their pupils. Overall, an expanded, mixed middle class 'patronises a public school system that is internally differentiated by race but also increasingly by class'.[15]

This crucial outcome of post-apartheid schooling is important in its own right, but is also an instance of a broader phenomenon touched upon in these pages. Chapter 1 argued that while the negotiated settlement delivered 'black' control of politics and continuing 'white' dominance of the economy, large-scale capital accepted the need to protect itself politically 'by developing alliances and class interest with aspirant black capitalists'.[16] Chapter 2 noted the ANC's commitment to fostering a black middle class and its use of increasingly prescriptive BEE mechanisms as a social greenhouse to speed the growth of such strata. The analysis in Chapter 3 of urban policies and trends showed that market logic ensures that property developers will focus on expensive new housing, retail outlets and offices for the well-off. Chapter 4 discussed the intensive privatisation of suburban security in response to real and perceived threats of crime. Middle-class suburbanites travel from homes bristling with high-tech security, or in gated communities, to 'fortified enclaves where work takes place as well as consumption and leisure. These zones are connected by road and transport systems that favour the wealthy.'[17]

There is no need to belabour the point. The most significant change in post-apartheid South Africa's social structure has been the deracialisation of its upper reaches. Members of a racially mixed middle class have been major beneficiaries of the post-apartheid dispensation, in ways that were intended and in ways that were not. The black middle class is 'notoriously difficult to measure', and definitions depend heavily upon somewhat arbitrary 'lifestyle' measures or household income levels.[18] Without entering the intricacies of these debates, it is possible to draw upon them for certain broad findings. At the outset, it is important to distinguish between a middle class, broadly defined, and a much smaller, much richer upper middle class.

• A wide-mesh definition of 'middle class' includes households earning between R5600 and R40,000 per month (at 2008 prices). This category includes salaried professionals such as teachers, nurses, civil servants and technicians, but also a sizeable portion of blue-collar, unionised workers – beneficiaries of employment equity laws.

- Between 1993 and 2008, this section of the population grew from 7.7 million people to 10.4 million: the number of Africans in this total more than doubled, from 2.2 million to 5.4 million. The number of whites fell by about a third (reflecting emigration and also a sizeable number who entered the upper middle grouping in these years). The proportion of Indians and coloureds remained largely stable.

- This broadly defined middle class did not grow much faster than overall population increase: in 1993 it represented 19.2% of the population and fifteen years later just 20.4%; its share of the total national income declined slightly.

- The most striking change saw an upper middle class (households earning over R40,000 per month) roughly treble in size from 0.4% of the population to 1.3%. This number included a substantial proportion earning much more: their wealth and power constitute them as an upper class. Since 1994, the size, social weight and economic dominance of this stratum have increased.

- Within the upper middle class, numbering just over half a million people, the number of Africans rose from only 19,000 in 1993 to 257,000 in 2008. These include managers and senior administrators in the public and private sectors, as well as the direct beneficiaries of BEE – the corporate black bourgeoisie.
- In a dramatic shift, the share of national income earned by this upper middle class rose in the same period from 17% to 32%.

The 'new black middle class' tells at least two different stories. One is a saga of large-scale but relatively modest improvement: the entry of families into housing that they own, their children into better-performing schools, their consumer horizons expanded. Their story is also frequently one of financial over-commitment and indebtedness. Their position – Joel Netshitenzhe points out – is frequently 'tenuous and insecure'. While these families have entered a lifestyle that places a high premium on consumption, 'unlike their white counterparts, these emergent middle strata do not have historical assets, and they have large nuclear and extended families to support'.[19]

The other story is more dramatic: its protagonists rich and powerful, its details sometimes luridly visible but often shrouded in secrecy. The narrative is driven by the formation of overlapping political, financial and corporate elites, yielding new answers to 'who rules South Africa?' It is not necessary here to rehearse the history of BEE since 1993 – the targets and codes and charters; the loans, share allocations and flotations, deals and directorships – as these have been closely studied elsewhere. The most obvious outcome has been at the apex of the process: the emergence of the BEE moguls, a remarkably wealthy and politically well-connected cluster of individuals. They move seamlessly between high political office and the upper reaches of the corporate world: think Sexwale, Ramaphosa, Phosa and Macozoma, or their counterparts appointed by the ANC to run the parastatals. Less immediately visible are the significant inroads made by black South Africans into the management and ownership of new companies, or into the boardrooms of older corporates. By 2008, 32.5% of 'senior and top managers in private industry' were black. Of course a great deal of corporate power remains in white hands, but the demographics of the private sector have changed considerably since 1994. Black ownership and control now penetrate different levels and sectors of South African capital. And, as they were for the BEE-lionaires, political connections and patronage have been crucial for the next layers of black financiers and managers.[20]

Mention is often made of 'white capital' and 'black capital' in South Africa. While this may help distinguish between older and new layers of the corporate hierarchy, it is a pretty blunt instrument for analysing the class composition and distribution of power in South Africa. It remains the case that political power is primarily vested in the ANC, with its mainly black support base; and that large-scale private capital still reflects white wealth and control. But these spheres of power are not incompatible or in constant conflict. Their respective elites, 'though disagreeing on lesser-order issues, agree upon major fundamentals or latter-day "common sense" centred around the functioning of the market economy'.[21] Political and economic power are probably more closely aligned, twenty years into ANC rule, than they ever were under the National Party. The impact of BEE and of the new black bourgeoisie in the economy has political implications: 'it has created a powerful political lobby inside and around the ANC against radical change.'[22]

Prospects for change?

If that is the case, does it mean that the shape of post-apartheid South Africa is now fairly clearly defined? How far into the future does one expect the '50% solution' – a stark division between upper- and middle-class beneficiaries, of all races, and the marginalisation of a largely black underclass – to hold? What would it take to refashion the contours of the political economy in more equitable, more inclusive, more participatory – and, in the long run, more sustainable – forms?

The ability of the ANC to effect such change is doubly

limited. First, there are profound weaknesses within the party itself. To the ANC's credit it has acknowledged these, in coruscating terms, in a document in the public domain. In the run-up to the Mangaung conference in 2012, a discussion document argued that neo-liberal influences were the source of 'subjective weaknesses' in the movement: 'The cumulative impact of all these weaknesses is the silent shift from transformative politics to palace politics wherein internal strife and factional battles over power and resources define the political life of the movement ... The political life of the organisation revolves around permanent internal strife and factional battles for power ... These circumstances have produced a new style of ANC leader and member who sees ill-discipline, divisions, factionalism and in-fighting as normal practices and necessary forms of political survival.'[23]

Secondly, and quite apart from the power-mongering and looting of resources by some of its members, the ANC's unity and coherence are also weakened by the inbuilt tension between its leadership – broadly at ease with elite enrichment, close to the mining–energy–financial conglomerates – and its grassroots members and supporters, kept onside thus far by the promise of jam tomorrow. There is a widening gulf between the ANC's 'transformative' rhetoric and its centrist policies. It is becoming increasingly difficult for the ANC to govern in a globalised capitalist economy *and* to represent the interests of its mass base.

These are real threats to the coherence and capacity of the organisation. Against them are vital strengths still enjoyed by the ANC. Because it can still tap a history of struggle and liberation, it remains electorally dominant; its visibility as government confers an extra layer of legitimacy; it is highly adept at mobilising its support base;[24] it retains control over state power and the concomitant patronage; and has thus far managed to keep tensions with its Alliance partners and own members 'in house'. Susan Booysen pinpoints this combination of strengths and weaknesses as 'Colossus in decline'.[25] Looking ahead, it is unlikely that the ANC can reverse its decline or mount a project of intellectual and organisational renewal.

Are there prospects for a post-apartheid politics to rekindle the impulses of the late 1980s and early 1990s – participatory democracy and a fairer economic and social order? There is a swathe of vacant political space, to the left of the ANC; and half a year into Zuma's second term of office, there appear to be two contenders to fill it. The first is the Economic Freedom Fighters (EFF), a political party deriving most of its profile from its leader, Julius Malema. He previously headed the strategically potent ANC Youth League; helped ensure Zuma's success at Polokwane; but was subsequently expelled from the ANC for his confrontational style and calls for the expropriation of white farms.

The EFF initially seemed merely a populism of bluster and bling, an opportunistic demand for access to resources by upwardly mobile but politically out-of-favour youth. But Malema is a master of the politics of gesture. Launching the EFF in Marikana deftly probed a wound where the ANC was already bleeding; and a creditable showing of 6% in the May 2014 elections showed that the EFF could tap reservoirs of frustrated hopes and anger. In parliament, its new MPs attended the chamber in red overalls and gumboots – visual shorthand for the working class – and their assault on Zuma ('pay back the money') wrong-footed and disconcerted the ANC.

Secondly, after years of speculation that a COSATU breakaway might form itself as a workers' party, this possibility hardened in 2014. COSATU was riven between critics of Zuma's leadership and union bosses loyal to the ANC president. Crucially, COSATU's largest affiliate, the National Union of Metal-workers of South Africa (NUMSA), decided not to support the ANC in the 2014 election, and to explore the prospects of a left-wing united front or possible socialist party. Whichever are the next steps that NUMSA takes, this notional new party – for all its challenge to the ANC – will find it difficult to define a political role. If it were to seek to represent unionised workers, it would have the same disconnect with non-unionised and casual workers, and the unemployed, that COSATU has experienced since 1994. And if it were to reach into shack settlements and the informal sector, it would risk losing the organisational muscle possessed by established trade unions. If the new party could find common ground with independent left groupings (such as the Democratic Left Front, the Workers and Socialist Party, and an array of activist NGOs), this could be a significant development. The left formations are tiny, but punch above their weight in contributing to progressive politics in South Africa. They play a vital role in political education and training, and as critics of the ANC–SACP's claims to speak 'for the people'. If these forces could coalesce in a politics of hope, and engage in 'the painstaking slog of building a genuinely democratic left movement',[26] the lineaments of post-apartheid politics would be redrawn.

Until an outcome on those lines, there is no political vehicle for poor South Africans. There are any number of political ideas and actions and aspirations among the poor; but they are dispersed between countless local associations, community organisations and NGOs. Their energies are considerable, but dispersed, evanescent and disconnected. Mobilisation of the poor is vigorous but shallow; it flares up frequently, but flickers out as often. Steven Friedman makes an important distinction between mobilisation and organisation: in the mass-based political resistance of the 1980s and early 1990s, he writes, 'although the mass movement against apartheid successfully mobilised poor people against the system, it did not organise them and so the grassroots poor entered the new democracy unorganised. The result is clear – a democracy in which the poor are able to choose the government they want but unable to be heard by the government which they choose.' There has been a lively national debate since 1994, he added, with a highly audible and organised multi-racial minority; while the majority, 'deprived of the organisation needed to be heard, are spoken about but do not speak. Predictably, neither social policy priorities nor the manner in which they are implemented reflect the concerns of the majority.'[27]

Friedman's point is vital. No party can speak for the poor unless it makes it possible for the poor to speak for themselves – and listens to them. Political organisations that give institutional form to the interests of workers and the poor, *and* have the social weight to challenge established parties, emerge infrequently in contemporary capitalist societies. Until such a politics takes shape in South Africa, the 50% solution will persist. For those at the wrong end of this equation, their lives will not be transformed; they will continue to be short-changed.

Notes

JCAS Journal of Contemporary African Studies
JSAS Journal of Southern African Studies
ROAPE Review of African Political Economy
SACQ South African Crime Quarterly
SAHJ South African Historical Journal

Introduction

1 John Iliffe, *Africans: The History of a Continent* (Cambridge: CUP, 1995), 187, 202.

2 Jeremy Cronin, 'How history haunts us', *Sunday Times*, 30 April 2012.

3 This account of social spending and redistribution is based on Jeremy Seekings and Nicoli Nattrass, *Class, Race and Inequality in South Africa* (New Haven: Yale University Press, 2005), 150–5; the quotation is at 356.

4 Representative of a much larger body of work are Glenn Adler and Eddie Webster (eds.), *Trade Unions and Democratization in South Africa, 1985–1997* (Johannesburg: Wits University Press, 2000) and Glenn Adler (ed.), *Engaging the State and Business: The Labour Movement and Co-determination in Contemporary South Africa* (Johannesburg: Wits University Press with Naledi, 2000).

5 Although this was recognised at the time by Johann Maree: 'There is a remarkably strong corporatist current flowing in South Africa. The major actors – labour, capital and the state – are so caught up in that they are hardly aware ... that they have become part of the current.' Johann Maree, 'Trade unions and corporatism in South

Africa', *Transformation* 21 (1993), 24.

6 David Lewis and Jay Naidoo, 'Social partnership in South Africa: Is it a sustainable mode of governance?', in G. Maharaj (ed.), *Between Unity and Diversity: South Africa and the National Question* (Cape Town: David Philip, 1999), 216.

7 Hein Marais, *South Africa Pushed to the Limit: The Political Economy of Change* (London: Zed Books, 2011), 444.

8 Karl Marx, *The Eighteenth Brumaire of Louis Napoleon*, first published 1852.

9 Letter by Dr Rodney Warwick, *Cape Times*, 29 January 2013 in response to my 'Our past haunts our future', *Cape Times*, 23 January 2013.

Chapter 1

1 Patti Waldmeir, *Anatomy of a Miracle: The End of Apartheid and the Birth of the New South Africa* (London: Viking, 1997), quotations are from dust-jacket, xiii-iv, 2–3, 250, 262.

2 Paragraph combines Hermann Giliomee, *The Afrikaners: Biography of a People*, 2nd edn (London: Hurst, 2011), 637, 648; and his *The Last Afrikaner Leaders* (Cape Town: Tafelberg, 2012), 14, 411–12.

3 Sampie Terreblanche, *A History of Inequality in South Africa, 1652–2002* (Pietermaritzburg: University of Natal Press, 2002), 102, 106.

4 Dale McKinley, *The ANC and the Liberation Struggle* (London: Pluto Press, 1997), 120; Patrick Bond, 'The South African economy', paper presented to Institute of Commonwealth Studies conference 'Looking at South Africa Ten Years On', September 2004, 1.

5 All quotes from Dan O'Meara, *Forty Lost Years: The Apartheid State and the Politics of the National Party 1948–94* (Johannesburg: Ravan Press, 1996), 402.

6 Thula Simpson, 'Toyi-toyi-ing to freedom: The endgame in the ANC's armed struggle, 1989–1990', *JSAS* 35, 2 (2009), 507.

7 Gail Gerhart and Clive Glaser, *From Protest to Challenge: Volume 6 – Challenge and Victory, 1980–1990* (Bloomington: Indiana University Press, 2010), 146.

8 See Peter Moll, *The Great Economic Debate* (Johannesburg: Skotaville, 1991); Ronaldo Munck, 'South Africa: "The great economic debate"', *Third World Quarterly* 15, 2 (1994), 205–17; Nicoli Nattrass, 'Economic restructuring in South Africa: The debate continues', *JSAS* 20, 4 (1994), 517–32.

9 MacroEconomic Research Group, *Making Democracy Work*

(Bellville: UWC, Centre for Development Studies, 1993). Nicoli Nattrass, 'South Africa: The economic restructuring agenda – a critique of the MERG Report', *Third World Quarterly* 15, 2 (1994), 219–26. She was, however, critical of its 'unconvincing and scary arguments' about the labour market and its failure to consider effects on business confidence.

10 Manuel quoted in Adam Habib and Vishnu Padayachee, 'Economic policy and power relations in South Africa's transition to democracy', *World Development* 28, 2 (2002), 245–63, 253; Erwin in Patrick Bond, *Elite Transition* (London: Pluto Press, 2000), 50.

11 Habib and Padayachee, 'Economic policy and power relations', 250.

12 Jo-Ansie van Wyk, 'Cadres, capitalists, elites and coalitions: The ANC, business and development in South Africa', Nordic Africa Institute, Discussion Paper 46, 2009, 24.

13 Terreblanche, *History of Inequality*, 95.

14 Cited in Van Wyk, 'Cadres, capitalists', 24.

15 Joe Slovo, 'Has socialism failed?' *South African Labour Bulletin* 14, 6 (1990); K. Coleman, *Nationalisation: Behind the Slogans* (Johannesburg: Ravan, 1999); Joe Slovo, 'Negotiations: What room for compromises?', *African Communist* (1992).

16 Quoted in Hein Marais, *South Africa – Limits to Change: The Political Economy of Transition*, 2nd edn (London: Zed Books, 2001), 95.

17 Paragraph based on Michael MacDonald, *Why Race Matters in South Africa* (Pietermaritzburg: UKZN Press, 2006), quotations at 178.

18 Carol Paton, 'SA's upper class "more African" – and ever wealthier', *Business Day*, 29 July 2013; Paton was reporting on a study by Jan Visagie, published by the economic policy forum Econ3X3.

19 Ibid.

20 Cited in Gillian Hart, 'The provocations of neoliberalism: Contesting the nation and liberation after apartheid', *Antipode* 40, 4 (2007), 678–705, 688.

21 Mike Morris, 'Who's in, who's out? Side-stepping the 50% solution', *Work in Progress*, 86 (1993).

22 William Faulkner, *Requiem for a Nun*.

Chapter 2

1   Mark Gevisser, *The Dream Deferred: Thabo Mbeki* (Johannesburg: Jonathan Ball, 2007), xxviii.

2   This story is told most fully in Anthony Butler, *Cyril Ramaphosa* (Johannesburg: Jacana, 2007), 253–319. The quotation is from 319.

3   In Gevisser, *Dream Deferred*; William Gumede, *Thabo Mbeki and the Battle for the Soul of the ANC*, 2nd edn (London: Zed Books, 2007); Daryl Glaser (ed.), *Mbeki and After: Reflections on the Legacy of Thabo Mbeki* (Johannesburg: Wits University Press, 2010).

4   Marais, *Pushed to the Limit*, 381.

5   Padraig O'Malley, *Shades of Difference: Mac Maharaj and the Struggle for South Africa* (London: Viking, 2007), 433.

6   Ibid., 470.

7   Anthony Butler, 'The state of the ANC', in S. Buhlungu et al. (eds.), *State of the Nation: South Africa 2007* (Cape Town: HSRC Press, 2007), 42.

8   William Gumede, 'Jacob Zuma and the difficulties in consolidating South Africa's democracy', *African Affairs*, 107, 427 (2008), 265.

9   Marais, *Pushed to the Limit*, 374.

10 Alec Erwin, 'The RDP Programme: A view from the Tripartite Alliance', *South African Labour Bulletin* 18, 1 (1994), 42.

11 Bond, *Elite Transition*, 115–18.

12 Quoted in Gevisser, *Dream Deferred*, 693.

13 A representative example of the discourse is the declaration adopted by the ANC's National General Council in 2005: 'we have now entered a new phase of our national democratic revolution … At the heart of this new phase is the challenge of promoting and accelerating sustained development and shared growth, spearheaded by a democratic developmental state' (cited by Van Wyk, 'Cadres, capitalists', 45).

14 Carol Paton, 'Amid the celebrations, the ANC still faces the same problems', *Business Day*, 21 December 2012.

15 Steven Friedman, 'Don't hold breath for a jump to the left', *Business Day*, 10 December 2012.

16 Susan Booysen, 'Plan's thought police undermine ANC's character', *Sunday Independent*, 28 April 2013.

17 Jonny Steinberg, 'Development as an alien culture', African Studies Association annual lecture, Oxford, June 2010, 24.

18 Susan Booysen, *The African National Congress and the Regeneration*

of Political Power (Johannesburg: Wits University Press, 2011), 8, 86.

19   David Everatt, 'Class formation and rising inequality in South Africa', in Moeletsi Mbeki (ed.), *Advocates for Change* (Johannesburg: Pan Macmillan, 2011), 71.

20   Booysen, *ANC and Regeneration of Political Power*, 480.

21   Steven Friedman, 'Vavi caught in proxy war', *Business Day*, 24 April 2013.

22   Carol Paton, 'The meteoric rise and the compromises of the SACP', *Business Day*, 16 April 2013.

23   Paragraph based on Sakhela Buhlungu, *A Paradox of Victory: COSATU and the Democratic Transition in South Africa* (Pietermaritzburg: UKZN Press, 2010), 105–13, 165–78.

24   Alexander Beresford, 'Comrades "back on track"? The durability of the Tripartite Alliance in South Africa', *African Affairs* 108, 432, (2009), 391–412; 'The politics of regenerative nationalism in South Africa', *JSAS* 38, 4 (2012), 863–84.

25   Booysen, *ANC and Regeneration of Political Power*, xiii, 211; Susan Booysen, 'The ANC circa 2012–13: Colossus in decline?' in John Daniel et al. (eds.), *New South African Review 3* (Johannesburg: Wits University Press, 2013), 39.

26   Report of the Secretary-General to National General Council, October 2010; cited in Booysen, *ANC and Regeneration of Political Power*, 117.

27   Carol Paton, *Financial Mail*, 21 May 2010; cited by Roger Southall, *Liberation Movements in Power* (Pietermaritzburg: UKZN Press, 2013), 268.

28   Anthony Butler, *The Idea of the ANC* (Johannesburg: Jacana, 2012), 78.

29   Moeletsi Mbeki, 'South Africa: Only a matter of time before the bomb explodes', *Business Day*, 12 February 2011.

30   Southall, *Liberation Movements*.

31   Booysen, *ANC and Regeneration of Political Power*, 22.

Chapter 3

1   Ivan Turok, 'Persistent polarisation post-apartheid? Progress towards urban integration in Cape Town', *Urban Studies* 38, 13 (2000), 2371. The sites of forced removals in, respectively, Johannesburg, Durban, Port Elizabeth, Pretoria, East London.

2   Alan Mabin, 'The dynamics of urbanization since 1960', in M.

Swilling et al. (ed.), *Apartheid City in Transition* (Cape Town: OUP, 1991), 40.

3 The account of the remaking of local government is based on Bill Freund, 'The state of South Africa's cities', in Sakhela Buhlungu et al. (eds.), *State of the Nation: South Africa 2005–2006* (Cape Town: HSRC Press, 2006), 305–9; and Alan Mabin, 'Local government in South Africa's larger cities', in Udesh Pillay et al. (ed.), *Democracy and Delivery: Urban Policy in South Africa* (Cape Town: HSRC Press, 2006), 135.

4 Andrew Siddle, 'Debate on municipalities vital', *Cape Times*, 3 January 2013.

5 Paragraph based on Freund, 'State of South Africa's cities', 312; Andrew Boraine et al., 'The state of South African cities a decade after democracy', *Urban Studies* 43, 2 (2006), 263–5; Alison Todes et al., 'Contemporary South African urbanization dynamics', *Urban Forum* 21 (2010), 333–5.

6 Doreen Atkinson and Lochner Marais, 'Urbanisation and the future urban agenda in South Africa', in Pillay et al., *Democracy and Delivery*, 23.

7 Loren Landau et al., 'The mobile nation: How migration continues to shape South Africa', in John Daniel et al., *The New South African Review 1* (Johannesburg: Wits University Press, 2010), 220.

8 Landau et al., 'Mobile nation', 220.

9 Todes et al., 'Contemporary SA urbanization', 337–9.

10 Bill Freund, 'Is there such a thing as a post-apartheid city?', *Urban Forum* 21 (2010), 296.

11 Boraine et al., 'The state of South African cities', 263–4.

12 Sarah Charlton and Caroline Kihato, 'Reaching the poor? An analysis of the influences on the evolution of South Africa's housing programme', in Pillay et al., *Democracy and Delivery*, 269–70.

13 Marie Huchzermeyer, *Cities with Slums* (Cape Town: UCT Press, 2011), 113.

14 Alison Todes, 'Urban spatial policy', in Pillay et al., *Democracy and Delivery*, 58.

15 Ibid., p. 113; Charlton and Kihato, 'Reaching the poor?', 255.

16 Charlton and Kihato, 'Reaching the poor?', 267.

17 Richard Pithouse, 'A progressive policy without progressive politics: Lessons from the failure to implement "Breaking New Ground"', *Town and Regional Planning* 54 (2009), 8.

18 Quoted in Catherine Besterman, *Transforming Cape Town*

(Berkeley: University of California Press, 2008), 51–2; Ivan Turok, 'Transforming South Africa's divided cities: Can devolution help?', *International Planning Studies* 18, 2 (2013), 169.

19 Njabulo Ndebele, 'Arriving home? South Africa beyond transition and reconciliation', in Fanie du Toit and Erik Doxtader (eds.), *In the Balance* (Johannesburg: Jacana, 2010), 58.

20 Paragraph based on Jo Beall and Sean Fox, *Cities and Development* (London: Routledge, 2009); Huchzermeyer, *Cities*, 26.

21 Pithouse, 'Progressive policy', 7.

22 This paragraph, and the two that precede it, are based on Huchzermeyer, *Cities*, 13–14, 182–3, 203–11, 215–21; Abahlali quotation at 215.

23 Peter Alexander, 'Rebellion of the poor: South Africa's service delivery protests – a preliminary analysis', *ROAPE* 37, 123 (2010), 37.

24 Steven Friedman, 'Beyond the fringe? South African social movements and the politics of redistribution', *ROAPE* 39, 131 (2012), 89.

25 Shaun Mottiar and Patrick Bond, 'The politics of discontent and social protest in Durban', *Politikon* 39, 3 (2012), see esp. 314–15, 320–1, 323.

26 Gillian Hart, 'The provocations of neoliberalism: Contesting the nation and liberation after apartheid', *Antipode* 40, 4 (2008), 682; Patrick Bond and Shauna Mottiar, 'Movements, protests and a massacre in South Africa', *JCAS* 31, 2 (2013).

27 Friedman, 'Beyond the fringe?', 87, 97; cf. Freund, 'Post-apartheid city', 287.

28 Paragraph based on Freund, 'Post-apartheid city', 288–9, 294–7, and Turok, 'Transforming South Africa's divided cities', 169–71.

29 Including Lindsay Bremner, *Johannesburg: One City, Colliding Worlds* (Johannesburg: STE Publishers, 2004); Richard Tomlinson et al., *Emerging Johannesburg: Perspectives on the Postapartheid City* (London: Routledge, 2003); Martin Murray, *Taming the Disorderly City: The Spatial Landscape of Johannesburg after Apartheid* (Ithaca: Cornell University Press, 2008); and *City of Extremes: The Spatial Politics of Johannesburg* (Durham: Duke University Press, 2011); Sarah Nuttall and Achille Mbembe (eds.), *Johannesburg: The Elusive Metropolis* (Durham: Duke University Press, 2008).

30 Bremner, *Johannesburg*, 18, 120–3, 129, 130–1, 132–3.

31 Ibid., 54–8; Murray, *City of Extremes*, 216–35.

32 Arjun Appurdai and Carol Breckenridge, 'Afterword', in Nuttall and Mbembe, *Johannesburg*, 354.

33 Graeme Gotz and AbdouMalik Simone, 'On belonging and becoming in African cities', in Tomlinson et al., *Emerging Johannesburg*, 128.

34 AbdouMalik Simone, 'People as infrastructure', in Nuttall and Mbembe, *Johannesburg*, quotations at 68, 75, 87.

Chapter 4

1 Antony Altbeker, *The Dirty Work of Democracy: A Year on the Streets with the SAPS* (Johannesburg: Jonathan Ball, 2005), 248.

2 Ted Leggett, 'The state of crime and policing', in John Daniel et al. (eds.), *State of the Nation: South Africa 2004–5* (Cape Town: HSRC Press, 2005), 159.

3 Stephen Laufer, 'The politics of fighting crime in South Africa since 1994', in Jonny Steinberg (ed.), *Crime Wave* (Johannesburg: Wits University Press, 2001), 16–17.

4 Ibid., 14.

5 Mark Shaw, 'Policing the compromise', in Steven Friedman and Doreen Atkinson (eds.), *South African Review 7: The Small Miracle* (Johannesburg: Ravan, 1994), 205.

6 Julia Hornberger, *Policing and Human Rights* (London: Routledge, 2011), 4.

7 Jonny Steinberg, 'Crime prevention goes abroad: Policy transfer and policing in post-apartheid South Africa', *Theoretical Criminology* 15, 4 (2011), 349, 351.

8 Jonny Steinberg, 'Security and disappointment: Policing, freedom and xenophobia in South Africa', *British Journal of Criminology*, 52 (2012), 349.

9 Leggett, 'State of crime', 164.

10 Ibid., 165.

11 Julie Berg and Clifford Shearing, 'The practice of crime prevention', *SACQ* 36 (June 2011), 24.

12 Steinberg, 'Crime prevention', 355–8; quotation at 350.

13 This and preceding paragraph based on David Bruce, *Marikana and the Doctrine of Maximum Force* (Johannesburg: Parktown Publishers, 2012), 14–25.

14 Ibid., 16.

15 See Julie Berg and Jean-Pierre Nouveau, 'Towards a third phase of

regulation: Re-imagining private security in South Africa', *SACQ* 38 (December 2011); Mark Shaw, *Crime and Policing in Post-Apartheid South Africa* (London: Hurst, 2002), 102–18.

16 SAPS Annual Performance Plan, 2011/12, cited in Andrew Faull, 'Towards a "new professionalism" for the SAPS', *South African Review of Sociology* 44, 2 (2013), 22.

17 Quotations from 1998 White Paper 1998 and SAPS *Community Policing Policy Framework and Guidelines* (1997), cited in Anthony Minnaar, 'The changing face of "community policing" in South Africa, post-1994', *Acta Criminologica* (2010), 193, 195.

18 Hornberger, *Policing*, 125.

19 Altbeker, *The Dirty Work of Democracy*; Jonny Steinberg, *Thin Blue: The Unwritten Rules of South African Policing* (Johannesburg: Jonathan Ball, 2008; Monique Marks, *Transforming the Robocops* (Pietermaritzburg: UKZN Press, 2005); and for the voices of police members themselves Andrew Faull, *Behind the Badge* (Cape Town: Zebra Press, 2010).

20 Clifford Shearing and Monique Marks, 'Criminology's Disney World: The ethnographer's ride of South African criminal justice', in Mary Bosworth and Carolyn Hoyle (eds.), *What Is Criminology* (Oxford: OUP, 2011).

21 Minnaar, 'Changing face', 197.

22 David Bruce, 'Good cops? Bad cops? Assessing the SAPS', *SACQ* 21 (September 2007), 15–20: the article is based on a longer report by the Centre for the Study of Violence and Reconciliation.

23 Jonny Steinberg, 'Crime', in Nick Shepherd and Steven Robins (eds.), *New South African Keywords* (Johannesburg: Jacana, 2008), 27.

24 David Bruce, 'Our burden of pain: Murder and major forms of violence in South Africa', in Daniel et al., *New South Africa Review 1*, 389–409.

25 Antony Altbeker, 'Murder and robbery in South Africa: A tale of two trends', in Medical Research Council, *Crime, Violence and Injury Protection* (Bellville: MRC, 2004); Anthony Altbeker, *A Country at War with Itself: South Africa's Crisis of Crime* (Johannesburg: Jonathan Ball, 2007), 48.

26 Shula Marks and Neil Anderssen, 'The epidemiology and culture of violence', in N. Chabani Manganyi and André du Toit (eds.), *Political Violence and the Struggle in South Africa* (Johannesburg: Macmillan, 1990), 29–30.

27 Gary Kynoch, 'Urban violence in colonial Africa: A case for South African exceptionalism', *JSAS* 34, 3 (2008), 645.

28 The broad case for a correlation between inequality and a range of socially undesirable features (violence, physical and mental health, drug and alcohol abuse, etc.) is made in Richard Wilkinson and Kate Pickett, *The Spirit Level: Why Equal Societies Almost Always Do Better* (London: Allen Lane, 2009). Altbeker was a contributor to the CSVR Report *Adding Insult to Injury: How Exclusion and Inequality Drive South Africa's Problem of Violence* (Johannesburg, 2008), 48–9.

29 Clive Glaser, 'Violent crime in South Africa: Historical perspectives', *SAHJ* 60, 3 (2008), 334–52; quotations at 347, 348. See also his *Bo-Tsotsi: The Youth Gangs of Soweto 1935–76* (London: Heinemann, 2000).

30 Bruce, 'Our burden of pain', 404.

31 Antony Altbeker, 'Who are we burying? The death of a Soweto gangster', in Steinberg, *Crime Wave*, 88.

32 Jonathan Jansen, *We Need to Talk* (Johannesburg: Bookstorm and Pan Macmillan, 2011), 4–5.

33 See the special issue of *Politikon* 39, 1 (April 2012) which analysed the discussions from various angles. (The transcripts are available at http://www.gcro.ac.za/project/non-racialism-ahmed-kathrada-foundation.) Quotations here from David Everatt, 'Non-racialism in South Africa: Status and prospects', 6.

34 Xolela Mangcu, *To the Brink: The State of Democracy in South Africa* (Pietermaritzburg: UKZN Press, 2008), 2, 102; T.O. Molefe, *Black Anger and White Obliviousness: How White South Africans Lost the Privilege of Being Heard* (Johannesburg: Parktown Publishers, 2012).

35 Paragraph based on Everatt, 'Non-racialism', quotations at 6, 13, 16, 19, 26.

36 Naboth Mokgatle, *The Autobiography of an Unknown South African* (London: Hurst, 1971), 349–50.

37 David Smith, 'In the rainbow nation, colour and class still count', *Mail & Guardian*, 9 September 2009; Njabulo Ndebele, 'Of pretence and protest', *Mail & Guardian*, 23 September 2009; Neville Alexander, *An Ordinary Country* (Pietermaritzburg: University of Natal Press, 2002), 117–18.

Chapter 5

1   Alan Hirsch, *Season of Hope: Economic Reform under Mandela and Mbeki* (Pietermaritzburg: UKZN Press, 2005), 72.

2   Thiven Reddy, 'Transformation', in Shepherd and Robins, *New South African Keywords*, 209.

3   Ibid., 210.

4   http://constitutionallyspeaking.co.za/what-we-talk-about-when-we-talk-about-transformation, 27 July 2009, 12 August 2010, 29 August 2011.

5   Reddy, 'Transformation', 219.

6   Steven Friedman, personal communication.

7   There is an extensive literature on South Africa's claims and capacity to be considered as a developmental state. A running commentary has been provided by numerous chapters in successive editions of the *State of the Nation* and *New South African Review* series; incisive overviews are provided by Marais, *Pushed to the Limit*, chapter 11; and Sam Ashman, Ben Fine and Susan Newman, 'The developmental state and post-liberation South Africa', in Judith February and Neeta Misra-Dexter (eds.), *Testing Democracy: Which Way Is South Africa Going?* (Cape Town: IDASA, 2010).

8   Adam Habib, *South Africa's Suspended Revolution* (Johannesburg: Wits University Press, 2013), 88, 93.

9   Ashman, Fine and Newman, 'The developmental state', 37.

10 Roger Southall, 'Can South Africa be a developmental state?', in Buhlungu et al., *State of the Nation, South Africa 2005–6*, xxv.

11 Robert Cameron, unpublished paper (2004) cited in Vinothan Naidoo, 'Assessing racial redress in the public service' in Adam Habib and Kristina Bentley (eds.), *Racial Redress and Citizenship in South Africa* (Cape Town: HSRC Press, 2008), 117.

12 Ivor Chipkin, 'Set-up for failure', in Habib and Bentley, *Racial Redress*, 129–52.

13 Marais, *Pushed to the Limit*, 143.

14 Linda Chisholm (ed.), *Changing Class: Education and Social Change in Post-apartheid South Africa* (Cape Town: HSRC Press, 2004), 7.

15 Ibid., 8, 18.

16 Roger Southall, 'Ten propositions about Black Economic Empowerment in South Africa', *ROAPE* 111 (2007), 70.

17 Vanessa Barolsky and Suren Pillay, 'A call for comparative thinking: Crime, citizenship and security in the global South', *SACQ* 27 (2009), 20.

18 Justin Visagie, 'The development of the middle class in post-apartheid South Africa' (2011) online at http://www.aceconferences.co.za/MASA%20FULL%20PAPERS/Visagie,%20J.pdf. See also Justin Visagie and Dorrit Posel, 'A reconsideration of what and who is middle class in South Africa', *Development Southern Africa* 30, 2 (2013); Justin Visagie, 'Who are the middle class in South Africa? Does it matter for policy?' online at http://www.econ3x3.org/sites/default/files/articles/Visagie%202013%20Middle%20class%20FINAL_0.pdf.

19 Joel Netshitenzhe, 'Competing identities of a National Liberation Movement and the challenges of incumbency', online at http://www.polity.org.za/article/competing-identities-of-a-national-liberation-movement-and-the-challenges-of-incumbency-2012-06-20.

20 Paragraph based on Southall, 'South Africa 2010', in Daniel et al., *New South African Review 1*, 11; and Southall, 'Ten propositions', 79–80.

21 Roger Southall, 'The power elite in democratic South Africa', in Daniel et al., *New South African Review 3*, 35.

22 Marais, *Pushed to the Limit*, 144.

23 African National Congress, 'Organisational renewal: Building the ANC as a movement for transformation and a strategic centre of power', online at http://www.anc.org.za/docs/discus/2012/organisationalrenewalf.pdf.

24 See Rushil Ranchod, *A Kind of Magic: The Political Marketing of the ANC* (Johannesburg: Jacana, 2013).

25 Booysen, 'The ANC circa 2012–13: Colossus in decline?' in Daniel et al., *New South Africa Review 3*.

26 Marais, *Pushed to the Limit*, 443.

27 Steven Friedman, 'Before and after: Reflections on regime change and its aftermath', *Transformation* 75 (2011), 8, 10.

Index

Printed in the USA
CPSIA information can be obtained
at www.ICGtesting.com
LVHW021412080923
756208LV00015B/155